MILITARY-TO-
Civilian
Career Transition Guide

The Essential Job Search Handbook
for Service Members

Second Edition

JANET I. FARLEY

JIST Works
America's Career Publisher®

Military-to-Civilian Career Transition Guide, Second Edition

© 2010 by Janet I. Farley

Published by JIST Works, an imprint of JIST Publishing
7321 Shadeland Station, Suite 200
Indianapolis, IN 46256-3923
Phone: 800-648-JIST   Fax: 877-454-7839   E-mail: info@jist.com

Visit our Web site at **www.jist.com** for information on JIST, free job search tips, tables of contents, sample pages, and ordering instructions for our many products!

Quantity discounts are available for JIST books. Please call our Sales Department at 800-648-5478 for a free catalog and more information.

Trade Product Manager: Lori Cates Hand
Production Editor: Heather Stith
Copy Editor: Chuck Hutchinson
Interior Designers: Amy Peppler Adams, Trudy Coler
Page Layout: Aleata Halbig
Cover Designer: Alan Evans
Proofreaders: Linda Seifert, Jeanne Clark
Indexer: Jeanne Clark

Printed in the United States of America
14 13 12 11 10 09   9 8 7 6 5 4 3 2 1

Library of Congress Cataloging-in-Publication Data
Farley, Janet I.
  Military-to-civilian career transition guide : the essential job search handbook for service members / Janet I. Farley. -- 2nd ed.
      p. cm.
  Includes index.
  ISBN 978-1-59357-731-5 (alk. paper)
  1. Career changes--United States. 2. Job hunting--United States. 3. Retired military personnel--Employment--United States. 4. Veterans--Employment--United States. I. Title.
  HF5384.F37 2010
  650.14--dc22

2009032412

We have been careful to provide accurate information in this book, but it is possible that errors and omissions have been introduced. Please consider this in making any career plans or other important decisions. Trust your own judgment above all else and in all things.

Trademarks: All brand names and product names used in this book are trade names, service marks, trademarks, or registered trademarks of their respective owners.

ISBN 978-1-59357-731-5

Dedication

*To uniformed service members and their families
past, present, and future.*

*Thank you for your selfless service and continued sacrifice
in times of war and peace, with hopes and prayers that you
experience more of the latter rather than the former.*

Acknowledgments

This book started with one good idea in 2004. With determination, relevant experience, requisite knowledge, and the support of others, the result was the *Military-to-Civilian Career Transition Guide*.

Five years later, the *Military-to-Civilian Career Transition Guide*, Second Edition, now rests in your hands. It is only because of the kind and gracious assistance of a number of individuals that this is the case.

Let me begin by saying that I remain grateful to all of those acknowledged in the first edition. Without it, this second edition wouldn't have evolved into its present state.

For this second edition, I wish to further acknowledge Lori Cates Hand, my editor at JIST, for her continued professional support and friendship over the years. Thank you, from my heart, for believing in this idea, having patience for it, and for making it a reality on the bookshelves. I am also grateful to others at JIST, specifically, Chuck Hutchinson for his editorial expertise; Amy Peppler Adams, Trudy Coler, and Aleata Halbig for their interior design and page layout assistance; and finally, Alan Evans for designing the cover of this book. Thank you.

On my desk there is a photo of a U.S. Army Staff Sergeant and a camel taken somewhere in the Iraqi desert. He sent it to me, along with his thanks, for writing JobTalk, a career advice column that appears in the European, Pacific, and Asian *Stars and Stripes* newspapers. I look at it everyday and silently thank him and all the other JobTalk readers for their letters and e-mail messages. This book was definitely written with them in mind. I also wish to acknowledge Heather Benit and Chad Stewart at OSD Stripes for allowing me the continued opportunity to write that column in the first place.

Thanks to Darla Huck, Contract Installation Manager at the Heidelberg Army Career and Alumni Program. I appreciate your time and updated information. Indeed, I appreciate all those working in the transition assistance centers across the Services. You are the first ones our military members and their families turn to as they begin to make the change from a military to a civilian life. Thank you for your expertise, your concern, and your willingness to go the extra mile for those who have gone the extra miles for us.

I am grateful to Terrance Gilbough and Kevin Sloan, who kindly offered up assistance as well. Best of luck to you both.

My gratitude is extended to Mimi Langenderfer, formerly of the Stuttgart Wounded Warriors Program, for the program information she provided me.

Thanks to Bill Scott and Craig Griffin of Bradley-Morris, Inc., for their kind assistance in answering my questions regarding military placement firms.

My various and much appreciated editors are forever graciously advertising my books. Thank you Victoria Locklair of *Civilian Job News,* Kissairis Munoz and Molly Wyman of *Today's Officer,* and Meredith Leyva of CinCHouse for your continued support and assignments! I am very proud to be associated with you and the good works that you do, on the job and off, for our military families.

I wish to also acknowledge the hard-working staff at Military OneSource/Ceridian, particularly Kerry Tucker, Pamela Smith, and Mary Craig for their endless efforts in support of our military families.

Finally, I'm eternally grateful to Farley, Frannie, and Terrie for their continued support, unwavering love, and tolerance of Chinese take-out, particularly when I'm in the writing zone.

CONTENTS

INTRODUCTION

Change is a concept that you live and breathe. It is one that will continue to stay with you as you transition professionally from the military to the civilian side of the house.

Will it be easy to make this big change in your life? The answer depends on you and on what you have experienced, how you have internalized it, and how you can use that to your future's benefit. I'm betting that, no matter who you are, the process won't be without its bumps in the road. It can be successful, however, if you make up your mind for it to be so from the beginning.

Like the first edition of the *Military-to-Civilian Career Transition Guide*, this second edition can help you

- Analyze the choices regarding whether you should stay in the military during these unique and challenging economic times.

- Prepare for what to expect from those around you as you transition from the land of ID cards to one without them.

- Identify your greatly expanded available military and civilian resources.

- Clarify your new potential benefits and entitlements as a soon-to-be veteran.

- Create an overall transition strategy that works.

- Identify your skills, strengths, weaknesses, and desires so that you can put yourself on the right career track.

- Write resumes and job search letters that get the attention of employers.

- Interview successfully for jobs.

- Effectively evaluate and negotiate job offers.

- Begin your new job with a clear understanding of the civilian side of things so that your next promotion is right around the corner.

Let this book be your companion in your transition. The *Military-to-Civilian Career Transition Guide,* Second Edition, was written by someone who has been there, done that, and got the T-shirt as both a military spouse for nearly 22 years and as a military career transition counselor for more than 8 years.

I can relate to the uncertainty, fear, excitement, and sometimes pain that accompanies a military career transition. Throughout the course of preparing the first edition, my husband and I experienced our own retirement transition from the military to civilian life. It wasn't easy. Things didn't always go as we had planned, but here we are five years later, alive, thriving personally, and content professionally. We're living proof that life does indeed continue after you take off the uniform, but you have to be able to withstand the twists and turns that you may not initially expect. You can't let them sidetrack you; you just have to adjust fire and drive on. You've had a lot of experience doing that in your military career, no doubt.

It continues to be my sincere hope that you take full advantage of all the resources and services available to you as you begin this new chapter in your life, including the use of this revised book. The number of changes in the benefits and resources landscape over the past few years is amazing. Some of those changes have been long, long overdue. Use them now to your fullest advantage. You worked hard for them. You sacrificed for them. You are due them. I have tried to accurately reflect them in this book; however, changes happen all the time. Always double-check at the source for the most up-to-date information.

Your new job and new life outside the military may be your focused goal for the moment, but don't forget to enjoy the everyday journey along your way to it, stress and all. After all, it is that journey that we ultimately look back on one day when we're old and gray and remember as that thing we called our life.

Thank you for your service and sacrifice to our nation. Good luck to you in your next career, and God bless you.

Janet I. Farley
2009

CHAPTER 1

Act II, Starring You

Not just anyone is capable of answering the call to serve his or her country, but you did. You had your reasons. Perhaps you put on a uniform, like so many others, after September 11, 2001, when innocence was lost and a nation was somehow changed forever. Or maybe you signed up because it was your turn to follow in the footsteps of a parent or grandparent who served honorably before you. Perhaps a savvy recruiter convinced you it was your best career alternative at the time. You might have joined the military to offset the ever-rising cost of higher education or simply to become a student of life itself.

Whatever your reasons, altruistic or not, you answered the call to selfless service for our nation, and that makes you very special indeed. Pat yourself on the back.

You proudly served your country for however long your body, your mind, your soul, and/or the Department of Defense allowed you to do so.

And now you find yourself standing boldly in the wings, eagerly waiting to walk onto center stage for the next exciting act of your career. Maybe you wonder exactly how you're going to get there from here without really breaking a leg in the process.

The *Military-to-Civilian Transition Guide* stands ready, willing, and able to proudly serve you now, if you will let it.

Getting There from Here

Before you can successfully launch Act II of your career, you need to have a clear picture of where exactly you are now. It's crucial to the overall success of your transition. Never underestimate the clarity of a genuine vision.

In other words, you just can't get there from here if you don't know where *here* is in the first place.

Everyone has a story. What's yours?

- Are you an activated reservist who doesn't want to go back to the same old job? Maybe that job just doesn't exist anymore?

- Did you do something incredibly stupid or sorely misunderstood to change the upward path of your military career?

- Are you a Wounded Warrior facing a new kind of future, one you never expected to have to deal with before?

- Are you asking yourself the burning 10-year-point question: Should I stay or should I go?

- Do you get the feeling that you've gone as far as you can in uniform and it's time to give things a go in the civilian world?

- Could you be that too-young-to-truly-retire senior enlisted service member or officer who is nearing military retirement? Is it your time in the whole cycle-of-life theory to move on to a second career?

- Do you have another story altogether?

Everyone is different, making your transition unique despite some of the more common brushstrokes inherent to the process itself.

You may be leaving the military on a positive note or not. Whatever your situation, embrace it and be fully aware of it. Denial, although comforting to an illusory degree, never helped anyone deal with the core reality of matters. And now, more than ever, you need to be able to effectively deal with reality because it's not a pretty sight at the moment!

The Current Economic Environment

You've read the newspapers. You've watched the evening news or surfed the Internet news feeds enough to understand that the big picture is not as welcoming as it could be on the jobs front. You would be oh so correct.

In January 2009, the U.S. Department of Labor reported a 7.6 percent unemployment rate in the United States, the highest rate our country has seen in about 30 years. By the time you read this, people may think of those depressing figures as coming from the good old days.

Nearly 12 million people are unemployed and looking for jobs. When you take off the uniform, the number will jump to 12 million and one. To say the competition for jobs will be stiff is an understatement.

Companies left and right are struggling to survive and, in doing so, have had to lay off employees like never before. From Wall Street to Main Street and everywhere in between, people are losing their jobs, their homes, and any sense of security they might have once erroneously felt.

To be sure, the economic news and the forecasted outlook are grim. You must be fully aware of that fact before you let go of your current paycheck. In all honesty, if you have a choice in the matter, you may even want to re-evaluate whether now is the time to get out in the first place.

This isn't being written to discourage you; the facts are what they are in today's environment. You must be aware of them so that you can adjust your job search strategy if necessary along the way.

If you are sure it is your time to make this transition, for whatever logic keeps you warm at night, make up your mind that it will be a successful one. Your body will follow your mind, no matter what the evening news tells you.

Great Expectations

Once you've owned up to the current realities, economically and personally, you can begin to make your transition as smooth and as profitable for you and your family as possible.

You can accomplish this by doing the following:

- **Expect to be stressed.** Backwards, *stressed* spells *desserts*, which is far more enjoyable than being stressed. A well-prepared Italian tiramisu always outranks a migraine headache. Unfortunately, stress isn't spelled backwards in this case. Accept the brutal fact of life that you and yours will suffer the slings and arrows that accompany change in general regardless of how well you prepare yourself for it. Keep things in perspective and remember that this too shall pass. Nietzsche had it right: What doesn't kill you makes you stronger.

- **Create your own flexible transition plan and use it.** Your transition assistance office can help you prepare a DD 2648, Individual Transition Plan (ITP). You can look at this plan in one of two ways. It can be just another piece of paper that gets you out of the military, or it can be a genuine planning tool that helps you remember to punch all the right tickets on your way out the proverbial door.

- **Identify the potential military benefits available to you and your family and use them.** You will learn about most of your benefits via the transition assistance office or the Department of Veterans Affairs. There may be a host of other potential benefits due you through other channels. The point is that you have to know to proactively seek out the knowledge yourself, Grasshopper. See chapter 3 for more information.

- **Learn the business of finding a job.** To land your next job, you'll need to have more than just a firm handshake and a charming twinkle in your eye. The outplacement services offered by the military are world-class and should be used to the fullest. Doing so opens up valuable networking opportunities with other connected job seekers and with employers seeking to hire the likes of you. It also provides you access to career counselors who can help you craft resumes and cover letters and hone your basic job search skills. Even if you consider yourself well versed in the whole job search process to begin with, go anyway. You won't be sorry you did, and it's free.

- **Learn the skills necessary to help you manage and advance your new career.** Starting now, you are your own career manager. Your success, or lack thereof, will depend on how you conduct yourself professionally in your new job. See chapter

9 for the down-and-dirty details you'll need to make it sans uniform.

When you have a crystal clear picture of where you are professionally and the skills you need to work on or obtain to make the next chapter in your life a success, you're almost ready to walk out on that great big stage of life.

There's just one more thing to keep in mind.

It's Not Just About You

You'll find a number of obstacles, real or self-imposed, as you transition out of the military. Paperwork will be a real one, coming at you from all sides and requiring your signature.

You may find yourself wondering how good you look in a corporate blue or gray business suit. Thoughts of resumes, successful job interviews, and subsequent six-figure offers may dance in your head.

Or not.

Maybe you'll be temporarily paralyzed by fears of not finding a decent skill-appropriate job in today's tough economic reality. You might even slip into denial and put off doing the things you know you need to do out of such fear.

All those thoughts, feelings, and fears are completely normal. After all, you are about to embark on one of the greatest adventures of your professional career. It just doesn't get any more exciting than this!

It's all about you, right?

Wrong.

You may be the star of the show, but without the support of cast members around you, you're more likely to flop than fly as you try to wow the audience with your own signature style. Those around you will be the ones to pull you back down to earth or pick you up off the ground when you need it the most. And make no mistake about it. You will need support.

Let's be clear here. You are the one who wears the uniform. You are the one who is looking for the job and upon whom all eyes will focus in the near term.

You are not, however, the only one in this show.

Those with whom you work will either provide you with the real-world support you need and deserve to get your transition act together, or they won't. If they don't, you can reasonably expect to get handed all the jobs that no one else wants to do before you leave.

If your work situation is less than ideal, make an extra effort to take the high road on your way out. If you are fortunate enough to work with a supportive lot, buy them lunch and promise to keep in touch. They might be calling you for a job one day.

These people are not always just those you work with, either. Your best friend, your spouse, or even your kids can quickly let you know in subtle ways (or not) that your change in direction is not necessarily a welcome one for their personal security levels.

Leaving the military might mean yet another move for everyone. It may mean that your spouse has to quit his or her job and find a new one all over again. He or she may be quite adept at this by now, but that doesn't make it any fun in the first place. Your kids may be confronted with leaving their schools, their friends, and their basic comfort zone.

These kinds of changes, as you already know in your gut, don't always happen without casualties along the way.

Open and honest communication throughout your entire transition process will make the changes easier to handle for everyone.

Culture Shock 101

"Toto, I've a feeling we're not in Kansas anymore."

You, too, will come to appreciate that same feeling that Dorothy had in *The Wizard of Oz* when she realized the world she knew and understood was no longer.

The military, for all the good, bad, and/or indifference you may have experienced at different points along the way, was relatively self-contained and predictable.

Typically, your uniform, rank, insignia, haircut, and physical fitness gave others an immediate recognition of who you were and your place in the camouflaged food chain.

You knew where to go for what, and the rules were clear for the most part, even if you didn't always agree with them. You could depend on your paycheck every 1st and 15th of the month, certain you weren't going to be fired or laid off because of the bad economy. Your true buddies had your back covered, and you did the same for them.

That's just not always the case in Civilian-Land.

As a civilian, you can let your hair grow, get a ring in your nose, and gain those extra 10 pounds without a first sergeant or commander telling you to shave or shed them. You won't have to salute anyone ever again, and the local supermarket will want to see your driver's license, not your ID card, when you try to cash a check. Your neighbors may not like the fact that you built a view-obstructing fence in your backyard, but unless a homeowners' association rule has been violated, what are they going to do?

Life is different on the outside, and although you may welcome that change, don't be surprised when you find yourself missing the strange comfort zone you had in your old military one.

Chances are you may even find yourself in mourning over your new civilian status, even if you wanted to get out of uniform more than anything in the world. It's not uncommon at all to experience some or all of the stages of grief, such as denial, anger, bargaining, depression, and acceptance. To effectively manage these stages, you must establish attainable goals, communicate clearly and often with those around you, and diligently work your transition plan.

Perhaps the best strategy for dealing with any of these stages is to confront head-on any obstacles that come your way. Don't ignore potential problems that could fester and morph into nasty monsters.

Show Time

It's time. No more safely waiting in the wings behind a plush, velvety camouflaged curtain. It's time for you to boldly walk onto center stage and begin Act II, starring you. Don't worry about forgetting your lines or stage fright. You will be a hit because you own a unique skill set and an array of talents unlike anyone else. You have been a bold, audacious, risk-taking warrior in a period of time that will go down in the history books. Now it's time for you to pen your own civilian success story.

Break a leg!

CHAPTER 2

Your Transition Mission

Your mission, should you decide to accept it, is to create a highly effective and flexible military-to-civilian career transition strategy. You'll have a wealth of resources available to assist you in this life-altering task, if only you proactively choose to take advantage of them.

Lucky for you, this message won't self-destruct in 30 seconds, and no one will ever deny knowing you in the first place. The success of this mission, however, depends on you alone and your willingness to create and execute such a plan.

This chapter helps you establish a timeline of required and useful transition activities. Essentially, it suggests what you need to take care of and when. Furthermore, it clues you in on what to expect at the military transition office when you finally grace that doorstep with your presence.

Consider these your first and most important steps in a long process.

Establishing a Realistic Timeline

You should not be surprised to learn that timing is a key element in the career transition process. Equally unsurprising is the fact that your timeline and the military's aren't always the same.

You may have the luxury of time to plot and plan your big move. You may not. Either scenario doesn't personally excuse you from doing all the things you have to do regardless.

So when exactly should you start planning your transition from the military? It depends on your situation.

Scenarios to Consider

Consider the following scenarios and suggested starting points:

- If you plan to retire from the military, start thinking about the concept at least five years out. Actually visit your transition office when you are 24 months out. At that point, you can complete your mandatory preseparation counseling. Doing this allows you to identify those helpful service providers who can give you answers to your many questions before you get out.

- If you are voluntarily separating from service, your actual transition should begin at the 12-month mark or sooner if you find yourself stationed somewhere transition services are not readily available. If you know you are going to be deployed when your window of transition assistance opportunity arises, take care of it before you go downrange! You'll save yourself considerable stress in the process.

- If you are being involuntarily separated from the military, your timeline may not be as flexible as you would like. You might find yourself out of the service within one year, one month, one week, or 48 hours, depending on your circumstances. You don't always know how much time you're going to have to process your transition and begin your job search. Your future is in someone else's hands, and that's disturbing to say the least. If you find yourself in this situation, you simply have to do your best under the circumstances.

Suppose that you are going to be separated from the military because of a medical condition. You have a period of time when you are waiting to see what the medical board is going to determine about your case. The result could be that you have to exit the military within 90 days from the date of the approved medical message. On the other hand, the result could demand that you remain on active duty despite your situation.

You don't know, and you won't know until the findings are presented to you. In this case, as you wait for the results from the medical board, begin the process of writing your resume and researching the job market. Just assume you are getting out and plan accordingly. If it turns out that you don't go, you've lost nothing. You've completed a dry run for that time when you do transition.

This step is critical. Don't let your emotions hinder your clear judgment. You wouldn't do so while on duty; don't do so while planning your future.

A Suggested Timeline for Success

Ask five different people when you should do what in your transition, and chances are good that you will get five different answers. To make matters more complicated, each of those answers could be correct.

What you will find is that only you can decide your true transition timeline. No one can push you. Keep in mind, however, that should you choose to ignore or procrastinate on some topics, you could miss out on potential benefits and entitlements.

The following checklist offers you a basic schematic to follow as you move mentally from being in the military to being a civilian again. Some of the activities will apply to you, and some will not, depending on your own circumstances. Pick and choose what works in your case. You might even need to add a few areas to your own list. The point is to have a rough guideline to work with in the beginning and throughout the transition.

Transition Timeline

Time Out	Activity
5 years	Start thinking about the idea and exploring potential career options.
	Consider joining professional organizations that support your military service, offer networking opportunities, and provide career transition services, such as the Military Officers Association of America (MoAA), American Legion, or other service-specific associations.
1–2 years	Ensure your voluntary retirement will be accepted by your branch of service.
	Provide the personnel/transition offices with an approved copy of your retirement.

(continued)

(continued)

Time Out	Activity
	Schedule and attend the mandatory preseparation counseling at the transition office. Invite your spouse to attend with you.
	Attend a Transition Assistance Program workshop or a Disabled Transition Assistance workshop if applicable. Again, invite your spouse to attend it as well.
	Develop your flexible transition assistance plan.
	If you aren't certain about a career path, objectively assess your education skills and interests by taking a vocational interest inventory at your installation education center.
	Have a family meeting and jointly discuss and prioritize your career options, location preferences, and salary requirements.
	If you are stationed overseas and want to remain there, start the approval process now.
1 year	Begin assembling a civilian wardrobe suitable for employment. Clothes can be costly, so if you add the new pieces gradually, you won't suffer sticker shock.
	Determine your dates for permissive temporary duty (TDY) and transition leave. Your personnel office can help you.
	Start networking in earnest for a job. Everyone is fair game, so include friends, family, coworkers, neighbors, and friends of such.
	Write a basic resume and cover letter that you can edit along the way for various opportunities. Request your Verification of Military Experience and Training (VMET), DD Form 2586, now to assist in the process. (More on VMET later in this chapter and tips on resume writing in chapter 5.)
	Start attending job fairs. Gather leads and research on potential employers. Network.
	Start sending out feelers to select employers regarding your skills and availability.

Time Out	Activity
	Develop a backup plan just in case.
	If becoming a full-time college student is in your future, research program entrance, testing requirements, and funding options now.
6 months	Start applying for the jobs in full force. Tailor each resume and cover letter to each job. Don't whine about it; just do it. Use the expertise of transition assistance centers or counselors if necessary.
	Take care to manage your stress levels. Keep the concept of life balance in mind.
	Establish and/or review your financial plan to prevent any disruption of bill paying or diminishment of basic quality of life levels.
	If you are under obligation or wish to do so, join the reserves.
	If you seek federal employment, start creating your federal resume now. Each agency may have its own example of what works for it, but they all contain the same basic information. (More on federal resumes in chapter 5.)
	Continue networking for your next job.
	If you live in government housing, inquire about clearing procedures.
	Visit the education officer and clarify your educational benefits and entitlements.
	Clarify and put into place your transitional health care options. Schedule a preseparation physical even if you are not required to do so. Set up a final dental exam while you're at it. Do the same for your family members.
3 months	Continue your job search and interviews. Network like there is no tomorrow.
	If retiring, schedule and attend a Survivor's Benefit Plan (SBP) briefing. Your spouse should also attend.

(continued)

(continued)

Time Out	Activity
	Schedule an appointment with the transportation office to clarify options and arrange for shipping and/or storage of household goods.
	Set up an appointment with the finance office to determine eligibility for separation pay.
	Use the free services of the legal office to update your wills and powers of attorney.
	Attend a Veterans Affairs (VA) briefing, generally arranged through the transition office. You can also visit online at www.va.gov.
30–60 days	Research potential living locations, depending on the job offers. The family center's Relocation Assistance Office can help you as well as the community's chamber of commerce. If your new home is near a military installation, learn more about the area at www.militaryinstallations.dod.mil.
30 days	Review your draft DD 214, Certificate of Release or Discharge from Active Duty, prepared by the transition office, for accuracy. It must be perfect before you sign it.
	Inquire about unemployment compensation benefits if you are not already gainfully employed or scheduled to be.
	Review and photocopy your medical and dental records (and those of your family members) for your own files.
	If you're retiring, start coordinating the ceremony and after party.
	File your VA disability claim online at www.va.gov.
	Determine whether you are going to convert your Servicemembers' Group Life Insurance (SGLI) to Veterans' Group Life Insurance (VGLI). You may have other less expensive options.
	If retiring, begin the process of obtaining new ID cards for yourself and any eligible family members.

Your First Visit to the Transition Office

You've seen others walk through the door to the transition office only to leave it as a changed person. You've longed for the day to join the ranks of those who are leaving the ranks for civilian pastures.

Your time has come. Depending on your branch of service, the "transition office" may be known by a different name and situated under a specific office.

> **Army:** Army Career and Alumni Program (ACAP) (www.acap.army.mil)

> **Air Force:** Airmen and Family Readiness Center (www.militaryinstallations.dod.mil)

> **Navy:** Command Career Counselor at the Fleet and Family Support Center (http://nffsp.org)

> **Marine Corps:** Career Resource Management Center (CRMC)/Transition & Employment Assistance Program Center (www.usmc-mccs.org/tamp/index.cfm)

> **Coast Guard:** Work-Life Division-Transition Assistance (www.uscg.mil/worklife/transition_assistance.asp)

To locate any transition assistance office (however it is named) worldwide, hop on the Internet and access the Department of Defense TransPortal Web page at www.transitionassistanceprogram.com.

On your first visit to the transition office, you will either be scheduled for a preseparation counseling appointment or told to have a seat immediately at one of the available computers to take care of your transition on the spot. You may be directed online to TurboTap (www.turbotap.org) so you can begin developing your own transition plan online.

Regardless, your first goal is to obtain a completed DD 2648, Preseparation Counseling Checklist for Active Component Service Members, or the DD 2648-1, for Reserve Component Service Members Released from Active Duty.

In the process, you will achieve the second and also important goal of obtaining valid information that can help you make educated decisions about your future.

The Preseparation Counseling Checklist

At first glance (see the facing page), you might believe DD 2648 or DD 2648-1 to be yet another form that you have to fill out and sign to get out of the military.

It is, and it isn't. This eventually signed form becomes a part of your permanent personnel file and serves as a starting point to planning your transition.

It's possible that without this form, you won't be able to complete your final clearing process, making it a necessary ticket to punch.

The form itself is a long checklist that addresses all the important things you should manage in your transition process. It also includes useful Web addresses for important service providers.

You will be required to check Yes or No after each point to indicate your interest in obtaining more information on a given topic. It won't hurt you to check Yes on everything, even if something doesn't apply to you. Checking No will not prevent you from receiving an entitlement if you are honestly due it.

After you have been briefed, either by a counselor or computer program, you may be given an additional list of service providers and asked to sign the form. You will be given a copy; the transition office will keep a copy or two.

Each transition office may have its own procedures; just remember that you need to get this block checked off in your exit process without fail.

It's also important to remember that the burden of getting the answers to your many questions lies only with you. You are given the tools (the basic information and the service provider contact numbers), and it is up to you to get the answers to the questions you have.

If you happen to get answers that you question yourself, ask someone else for clarification. Following up is worth the extra effort, and it could mean the difference between receiving a benefit due you or not.

Let's look at the items on the form in a bit more detail.

PRESEPARATION COUNSELING CHECKLIST
FOR ACTIVE COMPONENT SERVICE MEMBERS
(Please read Privacy Act Statement below before completing this form.)

SECTION I - PRIVACY ACT STATEMENT

AUTHORITY: 10 USC 1142, E.O. 9397.
PRINCIPAL PURPOSE(S): To record preseparation services and benefits requested by and provided to Service members; to identify preseparation counseling areas of interest as a basis for development of an Individual Transition Plan (ITP). The signed preseparation counseling checklist will be maintained in the Service member's official personnel file. Title 10, USC 1142, requires that not later than 90 days before the date of separation, preseparation counseling for Service members be made available.
ROUTINE USE(S): None.
DISCLOSURE: Voluntary; however, it will not be possible to initiate preseparation services or develop an Individual Transition Plan (ITP) for a Service member if the information is not provided.

SECTION II - PERSONAL INFORMATION *(To be filled out by all applicants)*

1. NAME *(Last, First, Middle Initial)*		2. SSN	3. GRADE

4. SERVICE *(X one)*	5. DUTY STATION	6. ANTICIPATED DATE OF SEPARATION *(YYYYMMDD)*	I am *(X one)*
☐ ARMY ☐ AIR FORCE			☐ Retiring
☐ MARINE CORPS ☐ COAST GUARD			☐ Separating Voluntarily
☐ NAVY			☐ Separating Involuntarily

7. DATE CHECKLIST PREPARED *(YYYYMMDD)*	7.a. Place an X in this box ONLY if you have less than 90 days remaining on active duty before separation or retirement. Please read the following instructions: If voluntarily separating or retiring and you have less than 90 days remaining on active duty before your separation or retirement, why was your preseparation counseling not conducted earlier? Please go to Section V - REMARKS and check the response that best describes the reason why preseparation counseling was not conducted earlier. ☐

SECTION III. ALL TRANSITIONING SERVICE MEMBERS MUST READ INSTRUCTIONS, SIGN AND DATE.

a. Items checked "YES" are mandatory for Service member to receive further information or counseling, or attend additional workshops, briefings, classes, etc. Service members that check "YES" in Item 11.a. will be released by Commanders to attend the appropriate workshop, briefing, etc. in its entirety.
b. Shaded Areas: Areas that are shaded mean (1) the information is not applicable or (2) the information is referring to a Web site address and the URL requires no explanation. For example: 11.b. is shaded under SPOUSE because DD Form 2586 does not apply to spouses. Items 11.f.(1) and (2) are shaded because they refer to Web site addresses and they require no explanation.
c. POST GOVERNMENT (MILITARY) SERVICE EMPLOYMENT RESTRICTION COUNSELING (Item 19): Service members cannot decline this counseling. It is required prior to separation. Therefore, no blocks exist to allow Service members the option of checking "YES", "NO", or "NA". Transition/Command Career Counselors shall refer separating and retiring Service members to an installation legal office (Staff Judge Advocate or Counsel's Office) to ensure they receive a post government (military) employment restrictions briefing or counseling from an ethics official.
d. I was offered preseparation counseling on the above date (Item 7) on my transition benefits and services as appropriate. I understand that this preseparation counseling is provided to assist my transition process as required by Title 10, USC, Chapter 58, Section 1142.
e. I have checked those items where I desire further information or counseling. I have also been advised where to obtain assistance in developing an Individual Transition Plan (ITP).
f. I ☐ accept ☐ decline *(X appropriate block)* preseparation counseling. *(If you check the "decline" box, you are declining preseparation counseling only on those items on this checklist where you have the option of declining.)* Sign and date the checklist.

8a. SERVICE MEMBER SIGNATURE	b. DATE *(YYYYMMDD)*	9a. TRANSITION COUNSELOR SIGNATURE	b. DATE *(YYYYMMDD)*

SECTION IV. Please indicate *(by checking YES or NO)* whether you *(or your spouse if applicable)* desire counseling for the following services and benefits. All benefits and services checked YES should be used in developing your ITP. The following services and benefits are available to all Service members, unless otherwise specified:

	SERVICE MEMBER			SPOUSE			REFERRED TO
	YES	NO	N/A	YES	NO	N/A	
10. EFFECTS OF A CAREER CHANGE							
11. EMPLOYMENT ASSISTANCE							
a. Dept. of Labor sponsored Transition Assistance Workshops and Service sponsored Transition Seminars/Workshops							
b. Use of DD Form 2586 (Verification of Military Experience and Training)							
(1) Do you want a copy of your Verification of Military Experience and Training (VMET) Document? If yes, go to http://www.dmdc.osd.mil/vmet to print your VMET document and cover letter.							
c. DoD Job Search Web site http://www.dod.jobsearch.org							
d. Transition Bulletin Board (TBB) and Public and Community Service Opportunities http://www.dmdc.osd.mil/ot/							
e. Teacher and Teacher's Aide Opportunities/Troops to Teachers http://www.proudtoserveagain.com							
f. Federal Employment Opportunities							
(1) http://www.usajobs.com							
(2) http://www.go-defense.com							
g. Hiring Preference in Non-Appropriated Fund (NAF) jobs (Eligible Involuntary Separatees)							

DD FORM 2648, JUN 2005 PREVIOUS EDITION IS OBSOLETE. [Reset] Page 1 of 3 Pages
Adobe Professional 7.0

(continued)

(continued)

PRESEPARATION COUNSELING CHECKLIST FOR ACTIVE COMPONENT SERVICE MEMBERS	NAME *(Last, First, Middle Initial)*						SSN	

SECTION IV *(Continued)*	SERVICE MEMBER			SPOUSE			REFERRED TO
	YES	NO	N/A	YES	NO	N/A	
11. EMPLOYMENT ASSISTANCE *(Continued)*							
h. State Employment Agencies/America's Job Bank							
(1) http://www.ajb.org							
i. Career One Stop http://www.careeronestop.org							
12. RELOCATION ASSISTANCE *NOTE: Status of Forces Agreement limitations apply for overseas Service members.*							
a. Permissive (TDY/TAD) and Excess leave							
*b. Travel and transportation allowances							
13. EDUCATION/TRAINING							
a. Education benefits (Montgomery GI Bill, Veterans Educational Assistance Program, Vietnam-era, etc.)							
(1) http://www.gibill.va.gov							
b. Workforce Investment Act (WIA)							
c. Additional education or training options							
(1) Small Business Administration http://www.sba.gov							
d. Licensing, Certification and Apprenticeship Information							
(1) Department of Labor http://www.acinet.org							
(2) U.S. Army https://www.cool.army.mil							
(3) U.S. Military Apprenticeship Program https://www.cnet.navy.mil/usmap/							
(4) DANTES http://www.dantes.doded.mil/dantes_web/danteshome.asp							
e. Defense Activity for Non-Traditional Educational Support http://www.dantes.doded.mil/dantes_web/danteshome.asp							
14. HEALTH AND LIFE INSURANCE							
a. Transitional Health Care Benefit - for Eligibility Criteria and additional information go to: http://www.tricare.osd.mil or http://www.tricare.osd.mil/Factsheets/viewfactsheet.cfm							
b. Option to purchase 18-month conversion health insurance. Concurrent pre-existing condition coverage with purchase of conversion health insurance. http://www.tricare.osd.mil/chcbp							
c. Veterans' Group Life Insurance (VGLI) http://www.insurance.va.gov							
d. Veterans Centers http://www.va.gov/rcs							
15. FINANCES							
a. Financial Management (TSP, Retirement, SBP)							
b. Separation pay (Eligible Involuntary Separatees)							
c. Unemployment compensation							
d. Other financial assistance (VA Loans, SBA Loans, and other government grants and loans)							
16. RESERVE AFFILIATION							
17. VETERANS BENEFITS BRIEFING							
18. DISABLED VETERANS BENEFITS							
a. Disabled Transition Assistance Program (DTAP)							
b. VA Disability Benefits http:www.va.gov							

19. POST GOVERNMENT (MILITARY) SERVICE EMPLOYMENT RESTRICTION COUNSELING
Information on post government (military) employment counseling (restrictions on employment, imposed by statute and regulation) shall be conducted by Services as appropriate. Transition/Command Career Counselors shall refer separating and retiring Service members to an installation legal office (Staff Judge Advocate or Counselor's Office) to ensure they receive a post government (military) employment restrictions briefing or counseling from an ethics official.

20. INDIVIDUAL TRANSITION PLAN (ITP)

a. As a separating Service member, after receiving basic preseparation counseling information and completing this checklist, you and your spouse (if applicable) are entitled to receive assistance in developing an Individual Transition Plan (ITP) based on the areas of interest you have identified on this checklist. The preseparation counseling checklist addresses a variety of transition services and benefits to which you may be entitled. Each individual is strongly encouraged to take advantage of the opportunity to develop an ITP. The purpose of the ITP is to identify educational, training, and employment objectives and to develop a plan to help you achieve these objectives. It is the Military Department's responsibility to offer Service members the opportunity and assistance to develop an ITP. It is the Service member's responsibility to develop an ITP based on his/her specific objectives and the objectives of his or her spouse, if appropriate.

	SERVICE MEMBER			SPOUSE			
	YES	NO	N/A	YES	NO	N/A	
b. Based upon information received during Preseparation Counseling, do you desire assistance in developing your ITP? If yes, the Transition staff/Command Career Counselor is available to assist you.							

DD FORM 2648, JUN 2005

Reset	Page 2 of 3 Pages

PRESEPARATION COUNSELING CHECKLIST FOR ACTIVE COMPONENT SERVICE MEMBERS	NAME *(Last, First, Middle Initial)*	SSN

SECTION V - REMARKS *(Attach additional pages if necessary)*

Complete the following ONLY if you placed an X in Item 7a. See page 1, Section II, Item 7a.

21. My counseling was conducted 89 days or less before my separation or retirement because: *(X one)*

☐	MISSION REQUIREMENTS
☐	PERSONAL REASONS
☐	MEDICAL SEPARATION
☐	LEGAL SEPARATION
☐	CHANGE IN CAREER DECISION
☐	OTHER *(Please provide a brief explanation)*

DD FORM 2648, JUN 2005

Reset — Page 3 of 3 Pages

Section I: Privacy Act Statement

You probably won't take the time to read Section I because it seems to reflect the small, unimportant fine print. If you should glance its way, you'll see that it cites the authority, purpose, uses, and disclosure requirements of the form.

Section II: Personal Information

You start to actually fill in the form at this point, so you'll most likely be paying attention. In Section II, you print or key in your name, Social Security number, grade, service, place of release from active duty, anticipated date of release, and date the checklist is prepared.

Section III: All Transitioning Service Members Must Read, Sign, and Date

Read Section III carefully before you sign it. This section really includes the fine print, and what it says differs depending on whether you are reading the DD 2648 or DD 2648-1. Most notable in this section, you are given the option to decline preseparation counseling. Don't do it. Even if you are having a bad day and just want to go home, check Yes. Even if you did check No and declined it, you would still be counseled regarding some of the topics anyway. Play nice. Check Yes. Learn something. Sign and date the form.

Section IV: Services and Benefits

In Section IV, you are given the opportunity to indicate whether you want more information about a particular benefit or potential entitlement. There are a number of topics to consider. They are discussed in more detail next.

For Active Component Service Members (DD 2648):

10. Effects of a Career Change

11. Employment Assistance

12. Relocation Assistance

13. Education/Training

14. Health and Life Insurance

15. Finances

16. Reserve Affiliation

17. Veterans Benefits Briefing

18. Disabled Veterans Benefits

19. Post Government (Military) Service Employment Restriction Counseling

20. Individual Transition Plan (ITP)

Section V: Remarks (DD 2648)

21. Reasons for late counseling (if applicable)

For Reserve Component Service Members Released from Active Duty (DD 2648-1):

10. Effects of a Career Change

11. Employment Assistance

12. Education/Training

13. Health and Life Insurance

14. Finances

15. Veterans Benefits Briefing

16. Disabled Veterans Benefits

17. Soldiers and Sailors Relief Act

18. Individual Transition Plan (ITP)

Section V: Remarks (DD 2648-1)

Section V is blank, sans anything you choose to include on it.

You can read detailed information about each of the potential benefits and entitlements online in the Preseparation Guide at TurboTap on www.transitionassistanceprogram.com or by typing www.turbotap.org in your Web browser.

The important points are provided in the following sections, along with a little extra food for thought here and there.

Effects of a Career Change

Life is going to be different for you and your family sans the military. You will feel stress, and that is completely normal. You may even experience the grieving process as you separate from a way of life that, like it or not, has been an integral part of your world.

Let's be real. No one has to tell you or your family what stress feels like. With the high up-tempo climate that you have lived and considered normal for so long, you could probably write the definitive book on the subject yourself.

That said, transition time brings another shade of stress to your lives, one that should never be ignored. As you may already suspect, it isn't always a bad thing.

Healthy stress can propel you into action and force you to accomplish the important tasks you need to accomplish at this point of your career. It's the "fight" option on that whole "fight or flight" theory. Again, you could probably write the book on that one, too.

Unhealthy stress, on the other hand, sucks the life out of you and those you love. Not good. No one has to tell you that too much stress of either variety can negatively affect your health.

Reality says that you're going to experience both kinds. You have to be able to recognize the difference between the two and know how to effectively manage the evil twin of the set.

One way to tame that bad puppy is to have at your ready a customized stress management plan that includes your own support team. Your support team could be made up of family members, friends, or service providers such as these:

- Family Service/Support Center
- Chaplain's office
- Military Mental Health Care Facility
- The Department of Veterans Affairs
- Military OneSource
- Marine for Life
- Military Family Network

You can also combat stress with activities such as the following:

- Working out

- Going for a walk

- Delving into a creative process to occupy your mind and senses

- Talking things over with your spouse and family members

You can beat stress by separating yourself from it for a little while and clearing your head. At that point, you can look more objectively and not emotionally at the issue and develop options for solving it if possible.

Available Assistance

Finding your next job or career will be easier if you are well aware of the different tools available to you.

Employment Assistance

As a transitioning service member, you are able to take advantage of Department of Labor Transition Assistance Workshops and service-sponsored transition seminars and workshops. Offerings may vary by area, depending on the available expertise. Job seeker, take note: Use these free services even if you think you already know it all. Chances are, believe it or not, you don't know it all.

According to the U.S. Department of Labor, an independent national evaluation of the program estimated that service members who participated in a transition assistance program (TAP), on average, landed their new post-military jobs sooner than those who didn't use the program. In the program, you will learn how to conduct a successful job search, write resumes and cover letters, and network with others.

As you transition out, request a Verification of Military Experience and Training (also known as VMET or DD Form 2586). This official document verifies the military training you have had and assigns it recommended college-level credit. Your VMET can help you remember training that you've had that may belong on your resume. You can obtain a copy of your transcript at www.dmdc. osd.mil/vmet by logging in with your CAC card or military pay password.

As you will learn in the transition office–sponsored workshops, there are a number of places to seek a job.

For example, www.jobbankinfo.org, a feature of the U.S. Department of Labor–sponsored Web site Career OneStop, offers you an excellent starting point for finding your next job.

Another good resource is www.hirevetsfirst.gov, a Veteran's Employment and Training Service–sponsored Web site that will direct you to www.usajobs.opm.gov for government positions or to a number of mainstream job search sites such as the following:

- www.monster.com
- www.careerbuilder.com
- http://hotjobs.yahoo.com/
- www.defensejobs.com

In your job search, it may also be useful to access any number of veteran-friendly Web sites, such as www.corporategray.com, www.bradley-morris.com, or www.hireveterans.com. You can access such sites, as well as a host of others, from the www.hirevetsfirst.gov site. Those interested in teaching opportunities should visit www.proudtoserveagain.com.

Federal opportunities may be found at www.usajobs.opm.gov and at www.go-defense.com. As a result of your military experiences, you may possess valuable hiring preferences that can help you land a job faster with the government.

State employment agencies post their jobs on Career OneStop at www.jobbankinfo.org/.

If you are in the reserves and want to read more about re-employment rights, visit www.dol.gov/elaws/userra.htm.

To find out more about Employer Support for Guard and Reserves (ESGR), visit www.esgr.org.

Keep in mind that you may be subject to some employment restrictions after leaving the military. The legal office can provide you with details as they pertain to your situation.

Relocation Assistance

Moving. By now you're probably pretty good at it, but this move will be a bit different. You're not being stationed to yet another pinpoint on the map. You're leaving the military, and you could find yourself staying in the next "duty station" for a long time.

Your family center's Relocation Assistance Program (RAP) can help you by offering a number of services such as the following:

- Needs assessment and individual relocation planning

- Access to automated installation information on such programs as Military Homefront's Plan My Move feature (www.militaryhomefront.dod.mil)

- Access to workshops and counseling sessions focusing on stress management, preparation of moving budgets, and buying/selling/renting real estate

Your actual transition out of the military may or may not involve a physical move. You may not know one way or the other at this point, so plan to get all the details regarding your benefits and entitlements in this area.

Your installation's housing office is the place to get the straight scoop on your actual housing allowances and entitlements.

Following are some important things to consider on this topic:

- If you are retiring and find yourself living or working on or near a military installation, you may be able to take advantage of available benefits such as medical, dental, post exchange/base exchange (PX/BX), and commissary shopping.

- If you want to get an idea about future potential locations to live, an excellent resource to reference is Military Homefront's installations directory at www.militaryinstallations.dod.mil.

- Even if you're not retiring, military installations often represent viable sources of employment.

With any relocation, remember that *cost of living* is a big deal. You might be thrilled over a $90,000 a year job offer, but if that job is located in Northern Virginia or Washington, D.C., the offer might not be the deal it seems on the surface.

To compare the cost of living in two U.S. cities or internationally, visit the following sites:

Homefair: www.homefair.com

Sperling's Best Places: www.bestplaces.net/COL

Salary.Com: www.salary.com

Payscale: www.payscale.com/cost-of-living-calculator

Bankrate.Com: www.bankrate.com/brm/movecalc.asp

After you receive your orders to separate, you need to visit the transportation office to inquire about household shipment and/or storage procedures. As you well know, during peak travel months, it can be difficult to get convenient moving dates set up for you and your family.

The military will move you and your family back to your listed home of record free of charge. If you want to move somewhere else, the military will cover the cost up to the amount it would have cost to move you to your home of record. You (or perhaps your new employer?) pick up the rest of the tab.

If you are retiring, you are authorized to move once anywhere in the continental United States, compliments of Uncle Sam. If you live overseas and wish to remain there, you may request an extension of this benefit for a period of time. Consult your transition and/or transportation office for more information on relocation and storage of goods.

Maybe you are one of the brave souls who choose to drive the moving van yourself. If you decide to do a Personally Procured Transportation move (formerly known as the Do-It-Yourself move, or DITY), good for you. Know that you may move your household goods (HHG) using rental equipment or a privately owned vehicle (POV) or by hiring a commercial mover. Under this option, you can receive up to 100 percent of the Government Constructive Cost (GCC) or an incentive payment of 95 percent of the GCC. You can even be advanced an operating allowance to help offset any out-of-pocket moving expenses.

Another relevant topic within the relocation discussion involves such potential benefits as permissive travel (TDY/TAD) to house hunt or job hunt. You may or may not be permitted this benefit. Receiving it depends on how you are going out the proverbial door.

If you are leaving the military because your contract is up and you don't wish to renew it, you are not eligible for permissive TDY/TAD. The gig is up, and you're on your own.

If you are being involuntarily separated or your retirement is being extended without your blessing, it could be a different story. You may be eligible for a number of days, generally not to exceed 30 with extensions, in which to conduct your house and job-hunting activities.

If you are stationed outside the continental United States (OCONUS) and relocating back to CONUS or another OCONUS location, you may be able to squeeze a few more days out the situation.

If you are retiring, you could be authorized travel anywhere in the United States.

You also should look at any excess leave you may have accumulated. You may have the option of selling it back to the government. Keep in mind, however, that you will be taxed on the money you receive.

If you are retiring or going into the reserves, you should have future commissary and post or base exchange benefits.

Retirees wishing to live overseas may be required to pay additional country tax on items purchased at the commissary and exchanges through the installation's customs office.

Education and Training Assistance

High on your priority list should be a visit to the installation education center where you can learn about your VA educational benefits and how to take advantage of them.

Depending upon your unique situation, you and your family members may be eligible to receive educational benefits under any number of VA-sponsored programs to include the following:

- Post-9/11 GI BILL
- Montgomery GI Bill—Active Duty (MGIB-AD)
- Montgomery GI Bill—Selected Reserve (MGIB-SR)
- Reserve Educational Assistance Program (REAP)
- Veterans Educational Assistance Program (VEAP)
- Educational Assistance Test Program (Section 901)
- Survivors' and Dependents' Educational Assistance Program (DEA)

National Call to Service Program Educational programs administered by the VA usually have a deadline for use. For example, the Post-9/11 GI Bill allows you up to 15 years to use or lose it, whereas the Post-Vietnam-era Veterans Educational Assistance Program

(VEAP) and the Montgomery GI Bill (MGIB) programs must be used within 10 years of separation from active duty.

To find out more about your VA Educational Benefits, see chapter 3 or go online at www.gibill.va.gov, where you can easily access the VA form 22-1990, Application for Educational Benefits, and apply online for benefits.

The Department of Labor (DOL) is also one place you should visit as you transition, for a couple of reasons. One, it is the place to find out about local and state employment opportunities. The DOL is highly connected to the community. For you, that means it can help you network your way into a job. Two, it can point you in the direction of additional training opportunities such as the Workforce Investment Act (WIA).

If you want to continue the career you had in the military as a civilian, and it requires licensures, check out these sites for information:

Department of Labor: www.acinet.org

DANTES Certification Information: www.dantes.doded.mil

COOL: https://www.cool.army.mil or https://www.cool.navy.mil

Other services provided by your education center include testing (CLEP, ACT, SAT, GRE, GMAT, and other standardized tests) free of charge while you are active duty.

Test results may be valid for a number of years. So, even if you aren't planning to go back to school for that master's degree just now, take the GRE or GMAT while it's free.

As of this printing, the General Test of the GRE costs civilians $105, the Writing Assessment is $50, and the Subject Test is $130. The GMAT costs $250. There is always the dreaded possibility that you would need to take one or more of the tests more than one time. To explore this topic in more detail, log on to the Defense Activity for Non-Traditional Education Support Web site at www. voled.doded.mil.

If you don't know what you want to be when you grow up, the education center can offer you a number of vocational and interest assessments and inventories. It never hurts to consider alternatives.

Finally, before you transition from the military, request a copy of your transcript (see the following table). All those military schools and/or courses you attended will show up on it as well as the American Council on Education's recommendation of how many college credits they could be worth. Some colleges and universities will review and accept some of your military training for college credit, saving you time and money.

Service Branch	Request Transcription From
U.S. Army	https://aarts.army.mil
U.S. Navy	https://www.navycollege.navy.mil or https://www.navycollege.navy.mil
U.S. Marine Corps	https://www.navycollege.navy.mil https://www.navycollege.navy.mil
U.S. Air Force	https://www.au.af.mil/au/ccaf
U.S. Coast Guard	http://www.uscg.mil/hq/cgi/ve/ official_transcript.asp

Health Care and Insurance

Medical costs are an ever-increasing fact of life. If you haven't realized that fact yet, you most certainly will upon receiving your first doctor's bill as a civilian.

When you land a civilian job, your employer may offer a decent health insurance plan. It should be one of those benefits you seek in an employer.

Even if you are retiring and think you will have health coverage for the rest of your life, don't depend on it. You will, at a minimum, want to consider a supplemental policy, particularly if you are not living near a military health care facility that can offer you service when you need it. Don't rule out buying full coverage either, depending on your medical needs and the affordability of available plans.

Certain service members may be eligible for an extension of health benefits through the Transitional Assistance Management Program (TAMP). Care is available for a limited time. Tricare eligibility under the TAMP has been permanently extended up to 180 days.

The four categories of eligibility for TAMP include

- Those being involuntary separated from active duty and their families.

- National Guard and Reserve members, known as Reserve Component (RC), separated from active duty after being called up or ordered in support of a contingency operation for an active duty period of more than 30 days and their family members.

- Members separated from active duty after being involuntarily retained in support of a contingency operation and their family members.

- Members separated from active duty following a voluntary agreement to stay on active duty for less than one year in support of a contingency mission and their families.

How long an extension you receive depends on how long you have been in the service and the conditions of your separation. Certain service members being involuntarily separated with other than adverse conditions and having served less than six years of duty could receive 60 days of additional military medical coverage; those with more than six years could receive 120 days of extended health benefits.

At the end of the 60- or 120-day period, there may also be the option of purchasing extended transitional health care insurance. In this case, you would have 60 days after your initial transitional health care ends to purchase the Continued Health Care Benefit Program (CHCBP).

Active duty service members and their families enrolled in Tricare Prime who wish to continue their enrollment upon the sponsor's separation from active duty are required to re-enroll in the program.

If you don't fall into one of these categories or you're not retiring, you are an "all others." How special is that? You are not eligible to use the military medical treatment facilities or Tricare. You may, however, purchase extended transitional health care coverage (CHCBP) for up to 18 months of coverage. You have 60 days to enroll in it after your separation, and it will not be cheap, although neither would a stay in the hospital sans coverage. If you opt to purchase this coverage, it begins the day after you separate.

Contact Humana Military Healthcare Services, Inc., regarding the CHCBP. You can find it online at www.humana-military.com or call 1-800-444-5445.

If you are retiring, you must make it a point to meet with your health benefits advisor to review your available options for continued care. Tricare offers retirees the following three options when it comes to obtaining medical care:

- Tricare Prime

- Tricare Extra

- Tricare Standard

To find out the details on each option, visit www.tricare.mil/bcacdcao.

The Tricare for Life (TFL) option kicks in if a member or family member becomes eligible for Medicare Part A, whether due to a disability or turning age 65. For more information on TFL, visit www.tricare.mil/tfl.

Continued health care coverage could be very important to you under any circumstances, but particularly if you are expecting a child. If this is the case, make sure your insurance covers the infant from the date of birth to 12 or 13 days after birth because medical expenses are costly during this period.

Regardless of how you're leaving the military, be certain to avoid any lapses in health care coverage. All it takes is one bad accident to cost you thousands of dollars.

Survivors of service members who died while serving on active duty for a period of more than 30 days are entitled to Tricare benefits. For more details, visit www.tricare.mil.

VA Medical Care and Health Care

There have been a number of changes recently regarding eligibility requirements for VA medical care. The VA system is now designed to provide quality medical care for those who need it the most and who can least afford it. Those who need it the most will find unlimited medical care at no cost. Others will find it unavailable.

Eligibility for VA health care depends on a number of different factors including the type of discharge, length of service, income level, available VA resources, and the VA determination regarding any service-connected disability claims.

For more information about VA health care eligibility, visit www.va.gov/healtheligibility.

Life Insurance

Another issue to consider is your Servicemembers' Group Life Insurance (SGLI). The government will pay for an additional 120 days of life insurance coverage after you separate, whether you are retiring or not. If you are totally disabled at the time of your separation, SGLI coverage can continue, free of charge, for up to two years from your date of separation.

VGLI

After SGLI expires, it is up to you to find your own life insurance. One government-sponsored option to consider is Veterans' Group Life Insurance (VGLI).

VGLI is a five-year term insurance policy. That means that as you age, your cost to participate increases. At the end of five years, if you decide you no longer wish to have VGLI, you may convert it to a civilian life insurance policy.

VGLI is issued in multiples of $10,000, up to $400,000, and can be converted any time to an individual permanent plan (whole life or endowment) for any of the 54 participating insurance companies.

In most cases, the VA will send you notification within 30 days after you separate that you must make a decision regarding this benefit. It is your responsibility, however, to apply within the time limits regardless of receipt of mailed notifications.

VGLI applications can be found online at www.insurance.va.gov/sgliSite/forms/8714.htm.

Traumatic Injury Protection Program (TSGLI)

TSGLI is a disability rider to the SGLI program. If a service member, covered under SGLI, suffers losses due to traumatic injuries, TSGLI pays from $25,000 to a maximum of $100,000 depending on the type and severity of injury.

Family SGLI (FSGLI)

FSGLI is available for eligible family members of those in the active duty or Ready Reserve insured under SGLI. Coverage may be obtained for up to $100,000 or an amount equal to the service member's coverage, whichever is less.

For more information on TSGLI or FSGLI, visit www.insurance.va.gov.

Dental

Get your pearly whites examined and cleaned within 90 days of separating from the military. If you do not do this, be sure the dental clinic representative notes this fact in your dental records before you clear the facility.

The VA allows for a one-time exam and cleaning up to 90 days after your separation from the military, assuming you didn't do so within 90 days before your separation.

Dental care is different from medical care. Delta Dental ends when you leave the military. Your next employer may offer a good dental plan for you and your family. If not, many fraternal organizations offer access to dental insurance (and group life and health for that matter) at competitive rates.

Retirees may consider Tricare's Retiree Dental Program (TRDP).

The TRDP offers premium-based dental insurance for military retirees, members of the Retired Reserve receiving retired pay, unremarried surviving spouses, and dependents. You pay the full cost of coverage, and you get basic dental care and treatment to include diagnostic services, preventive services, basic restoration services, endodontics, surgical services, and emergency services.

The Tricare Dental Program is available overseas as well.

Post-Traumatic Stress Disorder (PTSD)

PTSD is a fact of life for some service members and their families. You might already know far more about it than you wish you did.

What you need to know, whether you have experienced it or not, is how to get help should you or someone you care about experience PTSD.

The following resources can help:

National Center for Post-Traumatic Stress Disorder (PTSD): www.ncptsd.va.gov/index.html

AmeriForce Deployment Guide: www.ameriforce.net/ deployment

Courage to Care: www.usuhs.mil/psy/courage.html

Military OneSource: www.militaryonesource.com

For Your Medical "To Do" List

As you transition out of the military, be sure to do the following:

- **Get a physical before you separate.** If you are retiring, you will be required to get a physical within four months of your retirement. If you are getting out as a result of a medical condition or if you are being involuntarily separated under certain chapter actions, you also will be required to have a physical. If you have any questions regarding your requirements in this area, contact your legal office for clarification. If the local facility permits it, all others, including family members, should get a physical even though it is not required. You and your family should take advantage of this free health care while you can.

- **Get copies of your medical and dental records and those of your family.** Military medical records (yours and your family's) will remain government property even when you are no longer wearing a uniform. You should have a good copy of them so your next physician can have the whole picture. With your consent, your records will then be transferred to the VA regional office nearest your separation address.

- **Visit the medical board liaison officer at your servicing medical treatment facility.** Be sure to do so if you believe you have a serious medical problem or service-related handicap.

Finances

Some important questions to ask yourself follow:

- **Do I have enough money saved to transition out of the military?** A careful review of your expenses and income is in order at this point. Create a budget if you haven't already done so and stash your cash rather than spend it. There will be a multitude of expenses during your career transition. You want to be ready for them! Visit the Family Service Center for help managing your transition finances.

- **What happens to the money in my Thrift Savings Plan (TSP) account?** Your TSP is a defined-contribution retirement and investment plan that offers savings and tax benefits. When you leave the military, you have several options. You can do the following:

  - Leave your money where it is in the TSP.

  - Receive a single payment by either transferring it to a traditional IRA or an eligible employer plan such as 401(k) or a civilian TSP account.

  - Request a series of monthly payments based on a dollar amount or on your life expectancy. All or a portion of the payments can be transferred to a traditional IRA or eligible employer plan.

  - Request a TSP annuity, but you must have at least $3,500 in your account to do so.

- **Am I eligible for any additional separation pay?** Chances are, if you are being honorably but involuntarily separated and have served six years on active duty, you will have something coming your way. Your finance office will be able to answer this question for certain. Generally speaking, separation pay (which is taxable) is authorized only if the following applies:

  - You have finished your first term of enlistment or period of obligated service, *and*

  - You have at least six years of service, *and*

  - You are separating involuntarily, *and*

  - You are not yet eligible for retirement, *and*

  - You are not separating under adverse conditions.

Separation pay is computed on the basis of 10 percent of your yearly base pay when you separate, multiplied by the number of years of active duty service you have.

- **Am I eligible for unemployment?** You may be eligible for Unemployment Compensation for Military Personnel (UCX). Eligibility depends on the state paying the claim; therefore, only the state can tell you how much your weekly income check, for a limited time period, would be. To use this benefit, you have to apply for it shortly after separation. You will need your DD 214, Social Security card, and resume. To locate your state's unemployment office, visit this Web site:

www.workforcesecurity.doleta.gov/unemploy/agencies.asp

- **How will my retirement pay be calculated?** The answer depends.

There are three nondisability retirement systems to choose from:

  - **Final Pay:** Applies only to those who entered the military before September 8, 1980.

  - **High 3:** Applies to members who first entered the service on or after September 8, 1980, and before August 1, 1986. Also applies to members who first entered the service on or after August 1, 1986, and chose to revert to High 3 plan by not accepting the Career Status Bonus (CSB).

  - **CSB/REDUX:** Applies to members who first entered the service after July 31, 1986, and chose to receive CSB and the REDUX retirement plan.

For further guidance in this area, log on to www.defenselink. mil/militarypay/retirement/calc/index.html.

Service members who become wounded, ill, or injured, on the other hand, may be medically retired. Retirement pay for being medically retired can vary and is determined only after a Physical Examination Board (PEB-Medical Board) convenes to determine the percent of disability and makes recommendations regarding whether the disability is permanent or requires periodic re-evaluation for up to five years, at which time a final retirement system determination is made.

Connect with your transition office and/or your Retirement Services Office to determine your eligibility for such pay and with your finance office to ensure that your updated address and banking information is on file.

- **If retiring and I elect SBP, how much will it cost me?** The answer depends on the level of coverage you choose. Visit your installation's Retirement Services Office or your transition office for more information. If you choose not to enroll in SBP (Survivor Benefit Plan), your spouse will need to sign off on the paperwork acknowledging the fact. For online information, visit these sites:

www.defenselink.mil/militarypay/survivor/sbp/

www.vba.va.gov/Survivors/

Military-related associations may also be able to provide you with objective information on the topic.

- **Do I know what salary range to aim for in my job search?** This is another important reason to have a grip on your finances. Chapter 8 offers you more insight on this topic.

- **What other types of financial assistance might be available to me?** The VA offers home loans, FHA Mortgage Insurance, plus business and rural loans. Visit www.va.gov and www. sba.gov for more information.

- **Does the finance office have my forwarding address so I can receive my W2 form next year?** Simply check with your finance office to ensure that it has the correct address.

- **What is my credit rating with the three major credit-reporting bureaus?** The Fair Credit Reporting Act (FCRA) requires each of the nationwide consumer reporting agencies to provide you with a free copy of your credit report, upon your request, once every 12 months.

To request your free copy annually, visit www.annualcreditreport.com or call 1-877-322-8228.

The individual agency addresses are included here should you need to contact them for a second copy or have questions:

  - Experian, 475 Anton Blvd., Costa Mesa, CA 92626; toll-free at 1-888-397-3742 or online at www.experian.com

  - Equifax, P.O. Box 740241, Atlanta, GA 30374; toll-free at 1-800-685-1111 or online at www.equifax.com

  - Trans Union Corp, 2 Baldwin Place, P.O. Box 2000, Chester, PA 19022; toll-free at 1-800-888-4213 or online at www.transunion.com

Protect Yourself from Identity Theft

In the military, you are often known simply by your Social Security number. If you are married to a military service member, you may not even remember your own number anymore because you are always required to give your spouse's for everything. Now more than ever, it is important to safeguard this all-too-freely-given information.

- Avoid having your Social Security number preprinted on your personal checks and always shred documents having it listed when you no longer need them.

- Never give your Social Security number or any personal information to anyone on the telephone unless you have made the call and know where it is you are calling in the first place.

- Keep your computer's security systems updated.

- When shopping online, use only secure checkouts. You can tell whether a site is secure by looking at the https: line in the browser's Web address. If there isn't an s after http, it is not secure. Safe shopping requires the https.

- Never give out your personal information over the telephone to someone who called you first or online. Learn to differentiate between bogus e-mails and real ones.

- Invest in a paper shredder and use it.

- Review your credit reports at least once a year to make sure there are no discrepancies. Request a free one at www.annualcreditreport.com.

Reserve Affiliation

If you have not served eight years in the military, you may be required to do so in a reserve capacity with a Reserve or National Guard unit or with the individual ready reserves.

Affiliation with a Reserve or Guard unit has its benefits. Some of them include extra cash, benefits, and promotion. You eventually get to retire with them if you choose to, and you might get the opportunity to continue your travel to foreign and exotic places.

If you have fulfilled your eight-year commitment, you may still elect to continue serving with a Reserve or Guard unit.

For more information, visit these Reserve Web sites:

U.S. Air National Guard: www.goang.com

U.S. Air Force Reserves: www.afreserve.com

U.S. Army National Guard: www.1800goguard.com

U.S. Army Reserves: www.usar.army.mil or www.goarmyreserve.com

U.S. Coast Guard Reserves: www.uscg.mil/Reserve

U.S. Marine Corps: www.marforres.usmc.mil or www.mfr.usmc.mil

U.S. Navy Reserve: www.navyreserve.com

Disabled Veterans

The Veterans Administration will play a vital role in your and your family's post-military life. Chapter 3 is a must-read. For now, suffice it to say that you probably have a number of potential benefits and entitlements available to you through the VA.

You need to be sure that you attend a VA briefing before you separate from the service. If one is not available in your area, go online to the VA Web site (www.va.gov) and read the Benefits section carefully. Even if you attend a briefing, everything is in black and white on the Web site.

The VA, like any worthwhile organization, continues to evolve over time in response to outdated and ineffective practices. Its job has always been a big one, and it just keeps getting bigger. Be sure to keep up with the changes as you experience them because they may well affect your future benefits as well.

Since January 2009, the Honorable Eric K. Shinseki, who served as Chief of Staff, United States Army, from 1999 to 2003, has taken the top spot at the VA. You can be sure any changes will be relevant, thoughtful, and in the best interests of our service members and their families.

In a nutshell, the VA believes that you entered the service in perfect health. If you exit the service in less than perfect health, you should be compensated for that difference. The VA makes an important distinction, however, among veterans with disabilities. Veterans having a service-connected disability fall under the mandatory classification of VA medical care. Those whose disability is nonservice connected fall under the discretionary classification.

You should apply for such benefits as you transition from the military. Even if you think you are not due any, apply for them. If you receive a 0 percent disability rating, you've established a baseline in the event that future illnesses or other disabilities rear their ugly heads. You can't see into a crystal ball, and future mishaps you experience might have origins in your past military life.

Another plus: Disability monies are not taxed after a certain percentage. If you are retiring, your retirement pay may be offset by any disability compensation you receive. The disability portion, however, will not be taxed, whereas your retirement pay might be affected. The exception to this at the time of this printing involves those having a disability rating of 50 percent or higher.

Depending on your situation, you may be eligible to a monthly restoration of some or all of any VA disability offset under the Concurrent Retirement and Disability Pay (CRDP) program. You do not need to apply for this automatic plan if you are eligible for it.

Another potential option is the Combat-Related Special Compensation (CRSC), which provides military retirees a monthly compensation that replaces their VA disability offset. For more information regarding eligibility, contact the CRSC for your service branch.

> **U.S. Air Force CRSC:** www.afpc.randolph.af.mil/library/combat.asp

> **U.S. Army CRSC:** https://www.hrc.army.mil/site/crsc/index.html

> **U.S. Navy/U.S. Marine Corps CRSC:** www.donhq.navy.mil/corb/crscb/crscmainpage.htm

> **U.S. Coast Guard CRSC:** www.uscg.mil/hq/cgpc/adm/adm1.htm

Disability monies may or may not mean a lot to you at this point in your life. After all, you are in your earning prime, right? You won't always be, however, and this source of income in later years might be beneficial to you. If you are honestly due it, take it. You can apply online at www.vabenefits.vba.va.gov/vonapp/main.asp.

In addition to disability compensation, there are other benefits such as VA home loans, educational benefits, and, as previously introduced, VGLI. These, along with others, are discussed in more detail in chapter 3.

The VA also sponsors a unique rehabilitation program called the Disabled Transition Assistance Program (DTAP) and a VA Vocational Rehabilitation Program. Your local VA representative or your transition assistance office can point you in the right direction if you're interested in these programs.

Individual Transition Plan (ITP)

As mentioned earlier in this chapter, the DD 2648 is a required form that becomes a part of your official personnel file. Public Law 107-103 states that all exiting service members must be informed regarding their potential benefits and entitlements. Completion of this form fulfills that legal requirement. After learning about your potential benefits and entitlements, you and your spouse, if applicable, are further entitled to receive assistance in developing an Individual Transition Plan (ITP). The purpose of an ITP is to identify educational, training, and employment objectives. It further aims to assist you in developing a plan to achieve those objectives.

Retiree Benefits

As you plan your eventual retirement, you should contact the installation's retirement services officer and/or the transition office, depending on where you are stationed, to schedule any available preretirement briefings. A multitude of topics ranging from how to obtain your retiree ID card, to facility and service availability, to survivor benefit plan elections will be discussed.

Leaving the Service: Important Points to Remember

As you plan to leave the service, don't forget the points discussed next.

Your DD 214

Everyone who leaves the military receives a DD 214, Certificate of Release or Discharge from Active Duty. This is an incredibly important document for which you must always maintain accountability.

Before you sign your DD 214, be sure it is 100 percent accurate. If you haven't already done so by now, assemble, in chronological order, all your certificates of training and military orders into one binder. When you review your draft DD 214, make sure everything (such as your education and awards) is included on it.

When you sign this form, it is final. It documents your entire military existence and will be an important form later when you try to use your VA benefits, obtain a federal job, vote, or obtain federal financial aid. It would be to your advantage to keep your original in a safe place, such as a safe deposit box. You may want to consider registering it at your local county courthouse. If you ever lose the document, you can easily obtain a copy there.

Military Records

You need to take special care of your military records.

- Make sure all your military records are in good order. Reviewing them and getting any inconsistencies or errors corrected now may be a hassle. It will, however, be easier now than later. Having correct information may truly matter at some point in your life. If you do find an error in your records at some point, you'll be required to provide a written request to correct the error within three years of its discovery.

- Before you get out, carefully inspect your collection of military awards, medals, ribbons, badges, and other insignia. If you are missing anything, visit your unit personnel office or your local installation exchange for assistance in replacing it. After you are out of the military, you can request assistance through your branch of service using the SF 180, Request Pertaining to Military Records forms, found online at www.vetrecs. archives.gov.

- If you feel as though you should have received a particular medal or ribbon and did not, contact your unit personnel office for assistance in locating the service regulations outlining eligibility requirements or simply get the information yourself and do the legwork. Replacement medals and ribbons can be obtained from the National Personnel Records Center for a small fee. The address is National Personnel Records Center, Attention: Military Personnel Records, 9700 Page Boulevard, St. Louis, MO 63132-5000.

Discharge Decisions

If you feel you are being discharged from the military unfairly, you can request a review of your situation. Each service has its own discharge review boards, which in turn have the authority to change or correct any discharge or dismissal from the service. The board, however, has no authority to address medical or general court martial discharges. You, your next of kin, or legal representatives have 15 years from the time of your discharge to make such an inquiry using a DD Form 293, Application for Review of Discharge or Separation from the Armed Forces. You can access this form online at www.veterans.ocgov.com/forms/DD-293.pdf.

Miscellaneous Tips

Take note of these last few details before you leave the military:

- If your transition involves relocating, provide change-of-address cards to your post office before you leave the area.

- Wherever you end up calling home, register to vote by contacting the county voting clerk.

- If you wish to wear your military uniform again, do so only for appropriate and honorable occasions.

At Your Final Out-Processing

Procedures for final processing, of course, vary from post to base. Usually, you can expect to receive your military clearing papers within 10 duty days of your availability date or active separation if not taking transition leave or permissive travel (TDY/TAD). After you receive these, you'll be tasked with getting the "good to go" check mark from a number of facilities and service providers. You have to hit the pavement now! If you don't know the hours of operation for the places you have to go to, call in advance. Save yourself the headache of having to make return trips.

You will be required to present your completed clearing papers at your final out-processing. You may have to present the following as well:

- Your updated ID card (keep in mind that the expiration date on your ID card must match the separation date on your orders).

- Your original medical and dental records (be sure you have already made your personal copies and copies for the VA).

- The result of your completed physical exam if you are retiring (this is usually a time-sensitive task, meaning that you must complete the exam not earlier than four months prior to your transition leave date but no later than one month before your retirement).

- DD 2648 or 2648-1 (ITP), which proves that you received your mandatory preseparation counseling.

- DD Form 2656, Survivor Benefit Plan election. This form is required only if you are retiring. (Your spouse, if you have one, will be required to have signed this form if you have elected not to take this coverage.)

- VA Form 21-526, the claim for a VA disability rating.

- If you are stationed overseas and wish to remain there after your separation, you will also have to show proof that you have applied for and received command approval to do so. Country laws regarding this topic vary. Check with your legal services for details concerning your situation.

Year One as a Civilian

The business of getting out is just one part of your transition mission. Planning for what happens next is equally important.

How do you see your first year out? Here are a few possible scenarios:

- You leave your office as an active duty service member on a Friday evening and show up again on Monday as a federal civilian employee. There's no downtime for you, the consummate type-A individual. Right back to work. A seamless transition occurs because you planned it that way well in advance.

- You are offered a number of jobs before you take off your uniform. You have the time to effectively evaluate each offer and make the best decision for yourself and your family. Call yourself a superstar.

- You decide it's time to take a career risk and start your own business from scratch. Maybe you have retirement pay as a backup, or you avoided losing all your investments in the financial debacle of 2008. It's tough at first, but you have been saving up for some time to try out this dream. No guts, no glory.

- You don't get a job right away. You waited a long time to begin your job search and are just now starting to piece together a decent resume. Denial was your security blanket. Unhealthy stress will now be your constant companion. You only hope something turns up soon before you are forced to accept a job for which you are grossly overqualified.

- You take a few weeks or months off to decompress. You've earned and can afford it. You want to know what it feels like to sleep in late for a change or perhaps grow a goatee for a total "new-you" look.

- You don't score a job right away, but it's not for lack of trying. Your spouse works, so you still have one paycheck to tide things over, and you're close to getting one. You can feel it.

- Your world was turned upside down in the military as a result of an injury on the outside or inside. You are in a stall pattern for now.

These are just a few of the possible scenarios. You need to imagine what your own first year might look like because it will be a reality before you know it.

That reality demands that you ask yourself the following questions:

- What are your immediate employment needs?

- Do you have a family you need to take care of and a mortgage you must pay on time?

- Do you have a sufficient financial cushion to allow you the luxury of time in your job search?

- Do you need to get hired as soon as possible to keep the money flowing comfortably?

There aren't any right or wrong answers here. Ideally, you can take your time to find that seemingly perfect job and not accept anything less. Reality, on the other hand, suggests that you may need to take a decent job, get used to being a civilian again, and discreetly continue your job search.

CHAPTER 3

VA Benefits and Other Opportunities

As a veteran, you are afforded a number of potential entitlements and opportunities through different agencies. Take the time to explore those offerings and take advantage of them. In recent years, they have been greatly enhanced just for you.

Your Veterans Benefits

In your postmilitary life, the Veterans Administration (VA) will play a larger role in the facilitation of various benefits and entitlements that may be due you upon your separation from the service.

To investigate or apply for these benefits, contact any VA office by calling toll free 1-800-827-1000. You can also visit the VA Web site at www.va.gov to learn everything you've ever wanted to know about them and more. Most of the required forms are available online, and you can apply for many of the benefits online as well.

Please note that every effort has been made here, as throughout this book, to provide you with the most accurate and up-to-date information concerning the subject at hand. As in life, however, the rules, regulations, eligibility criteria, and availability are subject to change. Always check with the VA or the benefit source directly for the most current information.

Eligibility for most VA benefits is based on discharge from active military service under other than dishonorable conditions. Some military personnel may even be eligible for certain VA benefits while on active duty when they have completed 90 days of service during wartime or conflict periods or two years of military service since 1980 or 181 days during peacetime. As a veteran, you have a myriad of potential benefits, and you owe it to yourself to examine them all.

To get into the VA system for the first time after release from active duty, you must send a copy of your DD 214, Certificate of Release or Discharge from Active Duty, along with your application for benefits. You can file your application and discharge paper with any VA regional office or now conveniently online at http://vabenefits. vba.va.gov/vonapp/main.asp.

Specifically, you have potential benefits in the following areas:

- Education and training
- Life insurance
- Home loans
- Disability compensation and pension
- Vocational rehabilitation and employment
- Re-employment benefits
- Unemployment compensation
- Medical care
- Dental care
- Family and survivors

Education and Training Benefits

A number of changes have been made to the VA's education and training offerings in the past few years, and more are likely. Make it your job to keep up with them.

Contact your education office before you leave the service to verify your particular benefits. Be certain that you have a clear understanding of what they specifically are, how long you have to use them, and whether you are able to transfer your benefits to your spouse or other family members should you opt not to use them. The answers will vary significantly depending on your specific situation.

Generally speaking, however, the VA pays monthly tax-free benefits to eligible veterans, dependents, reservists, and service members to help finance the cost of your (or potentially a family member's or members') education.

You can use your benefits for the following:

- Undergraduate study at a college or university
- Graduate study at a college or university
- Technical or vocational training
- Correspondence and flight training

You might also be able to qualify for a work-study allowance, apprenticeship/on-the-job training, or remedial course work.

As you leave the service, keep in mind that these benefits do not last forever.

Post-9/11 GI Bill

Benefits under the Post-9/11 GI Bill are payable only for training pursued on or after August 1, 2009. You may receive benefits for any approved program offered by a school in the United States that is authorized to grant an associate's or higher degree. You may also be eligible to receive tutorial assistance or up to $2,000 for the reimbursement of one licensing or certification test. If you transferred to the Post-9/11 GI Bill from the Montgomery GI Bill—Active Duty or Selected Reserves or from the Reserve Education Assistance Program, you may also be eligible to receive these benefits for flight training, apprenticeship, or on-the-job training programs and correspondence courses.

If you were a member of the Armed Forces on August 1, 2009, the DoD may offer you the opportunity to transfer benefits to your spouse or dependent children. Policy updates are ongoing in this area.

A special provision to the Post-9/11 GI Bill is the Yellow Ribbon Program. This program allows U.S. degree-granting institutions the opportunity to voluntarily enter into an agreement with the VA to fund tuition expenses that exceed the highest in-state public undergraduate tuition rate. Participating institutions may waive up to 50 percent of those expenses, and the VA will match the same amount.

According to the VA, only individuals entitled to the maximum benefit rate (based on service requirements) may receive this funding. Eligibility is defined as follows:

- Having served an aggregate period of active duty after September 10, 2001, of at least 36 months

- Having been honorably discharged from active duty for a service-connected disability and having served 30 continuous days after September 10, 2001

- Being a dependent eligible for Transfer of Entitlement under the Post-9/11 GI Bill based on a veteran's service under the eligibility criteria listed previously

To get the most current information published on the Post-9/11 GI Bill, visit www.gibill.va.gov.

Montgomery GI Bill—Active Duty (MGIB-AD)

The MGIB-AD program, also known as Chapter 30, provides up to 36 months of education benefits. In addition to certification/ degree programs, flight training, apprenticeship/on-the-job training, and correspondence courses, you may also use this benefit for approved remedial, deficiency, and refresher courses. You can use these benefits for up to 10 years following your release from active duty. Limited extensions may be available.

If you are still on active duty, you may be able to contribute up to an additional $600 to the GI Bill to receive increased monthly benefits. For this additional $600 contribution, you may get up to $5,400 in additional benefits. Cha-ching! Check it out.

Montgomery GI Bill—Selected Reserve (MGIB-SR)

The MGIB-SR, also known as Chapter 1606, may be an option for you if you are a member of the Selected Reserve, which includes the Army/Navy/Air Force/Marine Corps/Coast Guard Reserves as well as the Army National Guard and the Air National Guard. You can use this benefit for the same types of education and training as mentioned for the MGIB-AD benefit; however, the time limit for using these benefits differs. With the MGIB-SR, you have 14 years from the date of eligibility for the program, or until you are released from the Selected Reserve or National Guard, whichever happens first. Extensions may be possible.

Reserve Educational Assistance Program (REAP)

Established in 2005, REAP is for members of the Reserve Components called or ordered to active duty in response to a war or national emergency (contingency operation) as declared by the President of the United States (POTUS) or Congress. Certain reservists who were activated for at least 90 days after September 11, 2001, may be eligible for benefits or increased benefits. A $600 buy-up program (similar to the one mentioned for the MGIB-AD) may be available for those eligible for REAP.

Veterans Educational Assistance Program (VEAP)

VEAP belongs to you if you entered active duty between January 1, 1977, and June 30, 1985, and if you elected to make contributions from your military pay to participate in the program. With VEAP, for every $2 contribution you make, the U.S. government matches with $1. You have 10 years after your release from active duty to use your benefits. Limited extensions may be available.

Life Insurance Benefits

New and improved options are available for life insurance benefits, depending on whether you are active duty. This section describes the options relevant to veterans or those soon to be.

Servicemembers' Group Life Insurance (SGLI)

SGLI is a low-cost life insurance available to service members and reservists upon active duty. It is available in $50,000 increments up to a maximum of $400,000. When you decide to leave the military, you will have 120 days of continued SGLI coverage from the date of your effective out. If you are totally disabled at the time of separation, coverage continues for one year.

Of special note is the Traumatic Injury Protection rider under SGLI (TSGLI), which provides for payment to any member of the uniformed services covered by SGLI who sustains a traumatic injury resulting in severe losses. TSGLI is retroactive for members who sustain a qualifying loss as a direct result of injuries incurred on or after October 7, 2001, through November 30, 2005, in Operation Enduring Freedom or Operation Iraqi Freedom, regardless of SGLI coverage. TSGLI pays a benefit of between $25,000 and $100,000 depending on the injury. Coverage continues through midnight of date of discharge, but you generally have up to two years from the date of loss to apply for payment.

Veterans' Group Life Insurance (VGLI)

After SGLI, you have the option of buying VGLI, a lifetime renewal term insurance policy. The amount of VGLI you opt to purchase cannot exceed the amount of coverage you carried of SGLI. Premiums are age-based, meaning the older you get, the more expensive it is. You must apply within 120 days of separation or one year and 120 days if proof of good health is provided. Those on the two-year disability extension are automatically converted to VGLI at the end of the two-year period.

Family Servicemembers' Group Life Insurance (FSGLI)

FSGLI is life insurance that provides automatic coverage to the spouse and children of service members insured under SGLI. Spousal coverage is available up to a maximum of $100,000, but it cannot exceed the service member's amount of coverage. Premiums are age-based. Dependent children are automatically covered for $10,000 at no cost. Coverage terminates 120 days after the service member is released from active duty. The spouse may then convert his or her policy to a commercial one.

Service-Disabled Veterans' Insurance

Service-Disabled Veterans' Insurance (RH Insurance) is a policy having basic $10,000 coverage; a $20,000 supplemental policy is available if premium payments for the basic policy are waived due to total disability. You must apply within two years from the date of notification of your service-connected disability to receive this benefit. For the supplemental policy, you must apply within one year of approval of waiver of premiums.

Veterans' Mortgage Life Insurance (VMLI)

VMLI is actually a mortgage protection insurance issued to those who are severely disabled and have also received grants for Specially Adapted Housing from the VA. Maximum coverage under this plan is $90,000, and veterans must apply for the plan before the age of 70.

Home Loan Benefits

The VA will also assist you in your home ownership aspirations. Veterans with qualifying service are eligible for VA home loan services, including guaranteed loans for the purchase of a home, a manufactured home, a manufactured home and lot, and certain types of condominiums.

The VA also offers guaranteed loans for the building, repairing, and improving of homes. You may also be able to use this benefit to refinance an existing home loan. Note that "guarantee" does not mean "the VA actually loans you the money." You are still responsible for finding a lender. The VA merely guarantees the repayment of that loan up to a certain point if the borrower fails to repay the loan.

No down payment is required for most home loans. You must obtain a certificate of eligibility from the VA before you can claim such a benefit. Depending on the nature of your disability, you may also receive grants to have your home specially adapted to your exact needs.

If you are a Native American living on Trust Land, you may qualify for a direct home loan. There is no time limit for taking advantage of this benefit. If you have filed a claim for disability compensation with the VA, it may in turn waive the funding fee required for use of this benefit.

Disability Compensation and Pension Benefits

If you have a service-related disability and were discharged under other than dishonorable conditions, you may be eligible for disability compensation. The VA pays you, on a tax-free monthly basis, for disabilities incurred or aggravated during your time in service. Your entitlement is established from the date of separation if the claim is filed within one year from separation.

How much you are paid depends on how disabled you are deemed to be. In certain cases, you may even be paid additional amounts, such as when

- You have very severe disabilities or loss of limb(s).

- You have a spouse, child(ren), or dependent parent(s).

- You have a seriously disabled spouse.

Current rate tables are available online at the VA's Web site. To apply for these benefits, go online at http://vabenefits.vba.va.gov/vonapp or fill out a VA Form 21-526, Veterans Application for Compensation and/or Pension.

Transitioner beware. This form is a multipart, 23-page document. Even though you may not have to fill out every section on the form, you can be sure that you will need more than 10 minutes to fill it out correctly. I recommend filling out a hard copy of the form before you apply for benefits online.

Income from Special Separation Benefits (SSB) and Voluntary Separation Incentives (VSI) will affect the amount of VA compensation received. Likewise, if you're retiring, take note. Your military pay is reduced by any VA compensation received. There are exceptions to this policy, however. They can be found in the Concurrent Retirement and Disability Payments (CRDP) and Combat-Related Special Compensation (CRSC) programs.

Concurrent Retirement and Disability Payments (CRDP)

The CRDP program provides a 10-year phaseout of the offset to military retired pay due to receipt of VA disability compensation for service members whose combined disability rating is 50 percent or greater. According to the VA, members retired under disability provisions must have 20 years of service to be eligible for this potential benefit.

Combat-Related Special Compensation (CRSC)

The CRSC program pays added benefits to retirees who receive VA disability compensation for combat-related disabilities and have 20 years of service.

Disability Pension

The disability pension is an income-based benefit that is paid to veterans with an honorable wartime service who are permanently and totally disabled due to a nonservice-connected disability (or who are 65 years or older). There is no time limit imposed on you to apply for this benefit.

Vocational Rehabilitation and Employment (VR&E) Benefits

Veterans having a serious service-connected disability may be afforded such services as vocational and personal counseling, education and training, financial aid, job assistance, and, if needed, medical and dental treatment. The goal of this program, often referred to as Chapter 31, is to help eligible disabled veterans get and keep lasting and suitable employment.

To receive an evaluation for VR&E services, veterans must

- Have received or will receive a discharge that is other than dishonorable.

- Have a service-connected disability rating of at least 10 percent.

- Submit a completed application for VR&E services.

The basic period of eligibility for use of services is 12 years from the latter of the following:

- Date of separation from active military service

- Date the veteran was first notified by the VA of a service-connected disability rating

If eligible, you are then scheduled to meet with a Vocational Rehabilitation Counselor (VRC) for a comprehensive evaluation to determine whether you are indeed entitled to services. A VRC will decide whether you have an employment handicap based on the results of his or her evaluation.

Entitlement to services is established if a veteran is within his or her 12-year period of eligibility and has a 20 percent or greater service-connected disability rating and an employment handicap.

When an entitlement determination is made, you will work with a VR&E counselor to accomplish a number of goals:

- Select a VR&E program track from one of five tracks:

  - Re-employment (with a former employer)

  - Rapid employment services for new employment

  - Self-employment

  - Employment through long-term services

  - Independent living services

- Identify viable employment or independent living options
- Determine transferable skills and explore labor market and wage information
- Identify physical demands and other job characteristics
- Narrow vocational options to identify a suitable employment goal
- Investigate training requirements
- Identify rehabilitation resources
- Develop an individualized rehabilitation plan

To apply for this benefit, go to www.va.gov.

Re-employment Benefits

The Uniformed Services Employment and Reemployment Rights Act (USERRA) protects service members' re-employment rights when returning from a period of service in the uniformed services, including those called up from the reserves or National Guard. It specifically prohibits employer discrimination based on military service or obligation.

For military service over 180 days, you must apply for re-employment with your employer within 90 days from separation. If service is less than 180 days, shorter periods apply.

Among the job rights provided for in the USERRA are the following:

- It establishes the cumulative length of time that you may be absent from work for military duty and retain employment rights to five years. There are exceptions to this time period, however.

- It provides protection for disabled veterans by requiring employers to make "reasonable efforts" to accommodate the disability. Convalescing service members may have up to two years from the date of completion of service to return to their jobs or apply for re-employment.

- It provides insurance that returning service members are re-employed in the job that they would have attained had they not been absent for military service, with the same seniority, status, pay, and other rights and benefits.

- It requires that reasonable efforts be made to allow returning service members to receive refresher training or new training to upgrade skills to help them qualify for re-employment.

- It provides for alternative re-employment positions if the service member just can't qualify for the position he or she would have attained had military service not interrupted.

- It also provides that while performing military service, a service member is deemed to be on a furlough or leave of absence and is entitled to the nonseniority rights accorded other individuals on nonmilitary leaves of absence.

- It provides for health and pension plan coverage. If an individual performs military duty of more than 30 days, he or she may elect to continue employer-sponsored health care for up to 24 months with the realization that he or she may be required to pay up to 102 percent of the full premium. For those having fewer than 31 days of military duty, health care coverage is provided as if the service member had remained employed. Pension plans are protected.

For more information about job rights for veterans and reserve component members, see www.dol.gov/vets/programs/userra.

Unemployment Compensation

You may be eligible for unemployment compensation, which is administered by individual states as agents for the federal government. Unemployment income is temporary and is funded by employer-paid taxes. Eligibility is based on past wages, reason for job separation, and availability and job search requirements.

Our nation's recent economic turmoil has resulted in a run on individuals applying for unemployment benefits. As recently as February 2009, DOL Secretary Hilda Solis increased the weekly amount of compensation paid to eligible applicants, and in some cases, extensions of benefits have been granted. If you wish to apply for unemployment, visit your state's Department of Labor or access it online, where you also may be able to file for it.

Medical Benefits

The VA provides an extensive range of health care services to veterans. Such services include treatment for military sexual trauma and conditions potentially related to Agent Orange exposure, ionizing radiation, and other Persian Gulf hazards. To receive care, you must generally be enrolled in the program.

Combat Veterans

The VA provides free health care for veterans who served in a theater of operations after November 11, 1998, for any illness possibly related to their service in that theater.

If you were discharged from active duty on or after January 28, 2003, your period of eligibility for free health care is five years from your date of discharge from active duty.

If you were discharged from active duty before January 28, 2003, and were not enrolled as of January 28, 2008, your benefits are scheduled to end on January 27, 2011.

Dental Benefits

You may receive a one-time dental treatment if you were not provided treatment within 90 days prior to separation from active duty. You have 180 days to do this. This time limit does not apply to you if you have a dental condition resulting from service-connected wounds or injuries.

Family and Survivor Benefits

You know the deal. We're born. We pay taxes. And sadly, we will die at some point. Although your main focus may be on finding a job right now, you should dedicate some time to answering the question "How do I take care of my family after I'm gone?"

You'll want to address this question because the VA, DoD, and Social Security Administration offer your survivors a number of potential benefits and entitlements that could mean significant savings for them and peace of mind for you in the hereafter, knowing that you did your best to take care of your loved ones.

Some family members of disabled or deceased veterans are eligible for benefits such as the following:

- Educational benefits
- Home loan guaranty for surviving spouse
- Medical care for family and survivors

- Death pension
- Burial of spouse and eligible family members
- Dependency and indemnity compensation

To learn more about these potential benefits and entitlements, visit www.vba.va.gov/survivors.

Other Benefits

As a veteran, you may be eligible for the following benefits as well:

- State veterans' homes
- Homeless veterans' programs
- Civil Service Preference
- Overseas benefits
- Free state benefits such as
  - Camping
  - Hunting and fishing licenses
  - Disabled veteran automobile license plates
  - Boat trailer registration fees and taxes
  - Handicapped parking card
  - Watercraft registration
  - Tuition for family members for some state colleges and universities

Additionally, Veterans Service Organizations (VSOs) and other organizations that have partnered with them can assist you with your VA benefits and your transition to civilian life.

Other Opportunities

As you make your transition from the military to the civilian world, take advantage of all services and opportunities that may be available to you. In addition to those offered by the military and the VA, the options described next may interest you.

Workforce Investment Act

The Federal Workforce Investment Act (WIA) provides training and job search assistance. Individual states manage their own programs, but the federal government provides funding. If you are leaving the military and do not have a service-connected disability, contact your state employment services office to inquire about program eligibility and application procedures. If you are leaving the military with a disability, you may be eligible for other job training opportunities as well. You can find detailed information about WIA on your state's Web page on the Internet.

Licensing and Certification Information

Certain occupations have professional and technical standards and may require a license or certificate outside the military. If your career field falls into this category and you wish to continue in it as a civilian, you will need to meet those standards and earn official recognition to do so. This is called the *credentialing* process.

Licensure and certification are the two primary types of credentialing. Licenses, usually mandatory, are granted by governmental agencies to allow individuals to practice a specific occupation. State or federal laws dictate the standards. Certificates are usually optional and are generally granted by nongovernmental agencies, associations, or private companies.

Be aware that credentialing requirements may vary from state-to-state. Some states honor reciprocity, however. For more information, see the following sites:

Credentialing Opportunities On-Line (COOL):
Army: https://www.cool.army.mil
Navy: https://www.cool.navy.mil

America's Career InfoNet: Certification Finder:
www.careerinfonet.org/certifications_new/
default.aspx?ES=Y&

America's Career InfoNet: Licensed Occupations:
www.acinet.org/acinet/licensedoccupations/
lois_state.asp?by=occ&nodeid=16

Self-Employment Resources

In the past, the concept of self-employment was often viewed as a career aspiration of a select few willing to pour their body, soul, and mind into a good business idea. In today's environment, self-employment may be viewed more often as a livelihood necessity for some.

One thing is certain. Self-employment isn't for everyone. It may be for you if you have a healthy dose of realism mixed in with a dream or two and topped off with basic know-how and talent. Or it may be for you if you have the economic need to generate some type of income in this tight job market.

People who are self-employed often find themselves working longer and harder than their 9-to-5 counterparts. The cost of starting your business, depending on the nature of your venture, can be expensive. Many would-be entrepreneurs opt to begin their businesses on the side as they continue the drudgery of their full-time job. Businesses generally won't see a profit for at least six months to a year or even longer. Only you can decide which path is the best for you and your family.

To assist in researching this area, there are a number of resources available to you, not the least of which is the VA's VetBiz services. Learn more about them at www.vetbiz.gov.

Business.gov (www.business.gov) is also an excellent place to begin your planning process. Here, you will find a number of veteran-related resources to assist you in starting and financing your business.

As you plot and plan your entrepreneurial dynasty, consult the experts at the Small Business Administration (SBA; www.sba.gov). With its resources, you can begin to make educated decisions, prepare a business plan, secure funding, and launch your business.

Consider tapping into your own network of contacts and selecting a special mentor just for this process. To locate a group of retired business executives who do just that, see www.score.org.

Another good resource to consider is The Veterans Corporation (VTC), an organization that provides veterans (including disabled service veterans) with access to capital, bonding, and education. Learn more about this resource at www.veteranscorp.org.

You can't go wrong by joining your local chamber of commerce, either. After all, the business of a chamber of commerce is to attract business. You will expand your professional database and potential customer base by untold numbers.

If you think buying a franchise might be up your alley, get the scoop first at "Buying a Franchise: A Consumer Guide" available online at www.ftc.gov/bcp/edu/pubs/consumer/invest/inv05.shtm.

Wounded Warrior Resources

Depending on your experiences in the military, your civilian world may be totally unlike the one you and your family thought you would ever live in. Take heart. You are not alone, and there are resources available to assist you and your family. Use them. They are worthy. They are knowledgeable. They can help you and yours to make your future brighter. They exist to serve you because you have served us.

Specific DoD Web sites to note include the following:

Wounded Warrior Resource Directory:
www.woundedwarriorresourcecenter.com

The National Resource Directory:
www.nationalresourcedirectory.org

Service-specific programs include the following:

U.S. Army Wounded Warrior Program:
https://www.aw2.army.mil/index.html

Army Virtual Solider and Family Assistance Center:
www.myarmylifetoo.com

Marine Corps Wounded Warrior Regiment:
www.woundedwarriorregiment.org

Navy Safe Harbor-Severely Injured Support:
www.npc.navy.mil/CommandSupport/SafeHarbor

Air Force Wounded Warrior Program (AFW2):
www.woundedwarrior.af.mil

If You Are a Wounded Warrior

There's no explaining it, but fate has thrown you a nasty curve ball. You and your family may now find yourselves facing a life unlike one you ever imagined you would, perhaps one with changed roles, changed expectations, and an uncertain future. To say your circumstances feel overwhelming at times would be a gross understatement.

Where do you turn? How do you proceed? Will life ever feel normal again? Will you ever find yourself worrying about something as simple as finding a job again?

To be sure, you have questions that deserve answers. The cruel fact, however, is that some of those answers may not materialize when you want them the most.

Whatever hand fate has dealt you, it is yours to handle. Breathe in. Breathe out. Educate yourself on your resources. There are many out there. Use them. Accept that life is different and make it the best you can, just as you would under any circumstances. Your body may be changed, but your heart, your soul, and your mind remain intact and can grow from this experience if you will only let that happen. You know how to be strong. Now is the time for you to turn that strength on full speed—*you* being the operative word here.

Professionally speaking, when and if you're ready to go back to work, keep an open mind. You may be able to return to your chosen career path, or you may have to physically and mentally consider other possibilities.

Nothing is impossible if you believe in yourself.

If You Are a Caregiver

Maybe you find yourself on the other side of the equation, assuming the role of caregiver. As much as you may want to, you can't make everything the way it was before life changed, so don't even try. You can just be you. Be supportive and do your best, but remember to take care of yourself as well, emotionally and physically.

- Assemble a support team to give you backup.

- Don't be hesitant to seek professional assistance.

- Pace yourself. Accept that you can't do everything and be sure to take needed breaks.

- Reach out in your community or online and connect with other caregivers.

- Be realistic. Know your strengths and weaknesses.

- Take care of your own health.

- Get the whole family involved if possible.

- Educate yourself on your spouse's condition and the resources that can help you both.

- If you need to return to work, make alternative caregiver arrangements that you are comfortable with.

- Learn to plan ahead for emergencies and acquaint yourself with any employer benefits that apply.

- Research your extended care leave options through the Family and Medical Leave Act.

Caregiver Support Sites

Family Caregiver Alliance: www.caregiver.org

Lotsa Helping Hands: www.lotshelpinghands.com

Operation Life Transformed (OLT): www.operationlifetransformed.org

Not Alone.Com: www.notalone.com

National Family Caregivers Association: www.thefamilycaregiver.org

CHAPTER 4

Job Search Basics
You Need to Know

In case you carry any iota of doubt, relax. Landing a job after being in the military is more than possible. Depending on your chosen career path, it may even be easy. You certainly have to consider the current economic environment as you begin to objectively analyze your situation, but *consider* is the operative word here. Don't let the situation paralyze you.

You are a doer, and doers make things happen.

Look at this moment in time for the unique opportunity that it is. You have the chance now to do anything you'd like to do with your career and indeed with your life. You can choose to stay in your current career path, or you can boldly go where you have never gone before.

Although the task in front of you might appear overwhelming at times, take comfort in the fact that others have done it before you and will most certainly do so after you. Approaching this task may be new territory for you, but not for long.

You've surely heard this adage: Give someone a fish, and he'll eat for the day. Teach him to fish, however, and he'll never go hungry again.

This story may be well worn, but it's true. It's particularly true when it comes to finding a job. Once you know how to land a job, you'll always be able to do so in the future. And chances are good that this won't be the last time you'll call yourself a job seeker.

Surveys say that you will change jobs five to six times over the course of your lifetime. That seems like a strong enough case to learn the basics so that you can use them over and over again.

Job Search Myths and Realities

The Loch Ness Monster. The alligator in the sewer. The clueless guy who got out of the military and somehow landed a six-figure job and a corner office with a view on his first interview.

Are they realities or simply urban legends fabricated by some unknown person to create stress in our lives? No one knows for sure, but we do know that separating fact from fiction is important.

Fact or Fiction?: You will make more money on the outside.

Whether this statement is fact or fiction just depends! You must consider a number of variables here, including your particular career field and your level of expertise within that area. Supply and demand of a skill set, as well as geography, also play a significant role. The only way to separate fact from fiction in this case is to do your own research and run the numbers. You might be surprised at your findings.

Fact or Fiction?: You need to find the perfect job when you get out of the military.

Fiction! Chances are you won't find the perfect job *ever*. Perfect jobs don't exist. If you're lucky, you will find a job or continue in a career that provides you with professional and personal fulfillment most of the time. Don't make the mistake of glorifying life out of the uniform. Unless you become a slave to your own business, you will still have to report to someone else and maneuver the finer points of organizational politics.

Fact or Fiction?: After an employer hires you, you're stuck.

Fiction! Luckily, you're never stuck as long as you are able to exercise your free will. You can always get another job. That's one crystal-clear plus of being a civilian. You never have to wait for your service branch to cut your orders, telling you to move somewhere you don't want to go.

Fact or Fiction: You will lose all job security after you leave the military.

There is no denying that the military offers a level of job security that is pretty difficult to match. Paychecks come on a regular basis. Benefits are generally readily available. Service members and their families are usually well taken care of in those areas. You may lose many of those benefits, and if you equate them with security, the answer here is fact.

On the flip side, however, as a gainfully employed civilian, you have benefits, too. Depending on your employer, those benefits may be generous or not.

The secret here is really no secret at all. You need to identify what matters the most to you, in terms of how you define security, and make that a priority in your next position.

You can also increase your flexibility by developing your own security levels. You can do this in a number of ways. You can build up a healthy savings account. You can ensure that some of your benefits are not tied to your employment as a prerequisite when you do accept a position. You can also make yourself as indispensable as possible to your new employer. And, of course, knowing how to find another job never hurts, should the worst case happen.

Get a Job

Getting a job is more than just a feeling you have to have a job, but making the company truly believe you know how your skills, abilities, past experience, and training will benefit the company.

—Chris Babich, career counselor who specializes in assisting veterans

Getting Your Priorities Straight

Before you begin passing around your resume, take out a blank sheet of paper and write the answers to these questions:

- Where would you like to live after you leave the military?

- What job would you realistically like to have?

- How much money do you need and want to earn?

After you answer these questions, prioritize your answers. What matters most to you? Location? If so, pull out a map and draw a circle around where you want to live and focus your search on that area. Perhaps location takes a back seat to the actual job. If this is the case, certainly your options are greatly increased. Focus instead on what you have to offer versus what is available. Is money your driving force? If so, go for the bucks. Remember, though, that what constitutes a stellar salary in one geographical location doesn't necessarily hold true for another area. Always take into consideration that cost-of-living factor.

Is it possible to prioritize your desires and actually find a job that fulfills all three factors? Sure, but it's not likely. If you find that you are able to meet two of the three factors, consider yourself lucky.

Have your significant other, if applicable in your case, do the same exercise and then compare answers. You might find this to be either a real eye-opening exercise or a reaffirming one. If you find that your answers differ by a landslide, you might want to discuss the questions on a more in-depth level with one another. Life will be much easier for everyone in the family if you are both on the same page. If there is no meeting of the minds here, at least be prepared for an even more challenging transition. In any event, going through this drill will give you a starting point from which you can begin to structure your own job search campaign.

It's important to remember that you can change your answers along the way, if you find it necessary or desirable. Flexibility is a job search must, and it's to your professional and personal advantage to periodically re-evaluate your answers and revise them as necessary. Tunnel vision is not an asset here; realism is necessary.

Effective Job Search Strategies

Without question, those who have transitioned successfully before you have done so with a well-thought-out plan of attack. Others have done so on sheer luck. A combination of the two is unbeatable. The following strategies and exercises are certain to improve your probability for employment.

Think Like an Employer

Employers obviously want to hire the best possible candidates for their positions. That means they want to have someone come on board who is qualified and willing to do the job and is able to fit in with others in the organization. Take a look at the following list of other much-sought-after characteristics:

- Solid decision-making skills

- Ability to learn

- Flexibility, adaptability, and persistence

- Effective verbal and written communication skills

- Assertiveness

- Professional networking skills

- Basic computer literacy
- Knowledge of company's history and goals

Do you possess any or all of the preceding characteristics? If so, keep them in mind because you will draw on them for use in your resume and during your interview. If you feel that you are lacking any of these valuable traits, take the initiative to develop them. You won't be sorry. They are basic and universal skills that employers often seek.

Organize Your Job Search Campaign

You should consider your search for employment to be a job in and of itself. There is no question that finding a job requires a great amount of time, patience, and perseverance. The ideal is that you devote 40 hours a week to your job search efforts. Reality doesn't always support that ideal, however. Chances are you are still employed by Uncle Sam and you still have professional responsibilities that inhibit full devotion to your search. Rather than bemoan this point, work with it. The amount of time you spend looking for a job isn't nearly as important as the quality of time you spend on your search.

Organizing your job search means that you identify the tasks you will need to accomplish to become employed. You will need to do the following:

- **Schedule your job search activities just as you would an appointment on your calendar.** Make sure to correctly note names, job titles, addresses, and contact numbers. You are likely to need this information throughout the process of developing your leads.

- **Keep track of your initial contacts with employers and any follow-ups.** When the action starts happening, it can happen fast. You might find it helpful to make notes in your electronic organizer or physically on copies of your resumes and/or cover letters you send out, to remind yourself of whom you spoke with regarding what position on what date.

  You could also use a worksheet to log the activity, such as the example provided on the following page. Do what works best for you, but keep track of names, telephone numbers, e-mail addresses, positions sought, and your efforts toward securing employment. Doing so will assist you in your follow-up efforts and in expanding your professional network.

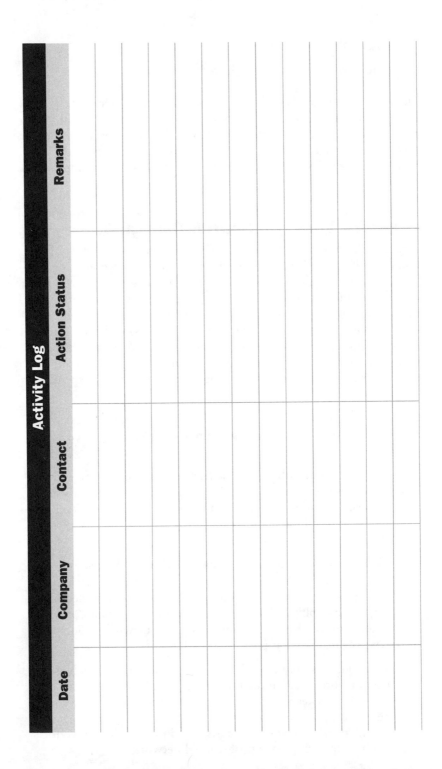

- **Set timelines for yourself.** For example, don't just say that you will draft a resume. Say that you will give yourself three working days to do it. Establishing a self-imposed deadline increases the likelihood of specific task completion. If you complete a bunch of little tasks, they most certainly will add up to a great big one, and before you know it, you'll be hired.

- **Re-evaluate your direction and progress on a regular basis.** This step is critical. You can't make good decisions using outdated information.

Be aware, however, that there is an inherent danger in organizing. Quite often, too much time is spent analyzing what needs to be done, and not enough time is spent actually doing it.

Tap into Available Job Assistance Resources

You're not on your own in this transition. A number of reputable resources, military and civilian, are available to assist you in finding your next job.

- **Military Career Transition Centers.** These resources were discussed in more detail in chapter 2. To locate the nearest one to you, go online to www.dodtransportal.org.

- **U.S. Department of Labor.** In addition to informing you about any unemployment benefits you may be eligible for, the employment office can refer you to employers for actual interviews, at no cost to you.

- **Military and professional associations.** By using your contacts within military and professional associations, you tap into the opportunity-rich world of the hidden job market. Here, jobs are filled before they are even announced to the public. If you aren't a member of any such groups, consider the benefits of such membership today.

- **College and university placement services.** If you have been attending school or plan to do so in the future, the placement services of your school can offer you job search advice and access to their employment database.

- **Executive search firms.** There are many search firms, and they all want your business. If you decide to hire a "headhunter," be sure you understand your financial obligation in the event you obtain employment while under contract with the firm.

Use of these services may or may not cost you. Read the fine print before you sign anything. You may be required to attend the firm's job search prep workshops and then specially arranged job fairs where you meet with representatives from its client companies. See more on using placement firms later in this chapter.

- **Employment agencies.** Employment agencies can help you land short-term, long-term, and, in some cases, permanent assignments with companies. Again, use of their services may or may not cost you. There are many reputable no-fee agencies that are ready, willing, and able to assist you. Generally, you are interviewed by a representative of the agency who will then refer and/or place you with other companies for a specific period of time. In such cases, you usually remain an employee of the agency and not of the company where you happen to be assigned. In other cases, you may be placed with a client company for a certain period of time, after which you may be hired directly by that company and relieved of your obligation to the employment agency.

The Truth About Military Placement Firms

A successful job search happens when you use all the available resources at your disposal. One such resource not to be overlooked is military placement firms. Too often, however, such organizations are given a bad rap by service members who assume that headhunters are just in it for the bucks. Let's be honest here. Any business wants to make a profit, so don't let that all-too-real fact of life throw you as you consider whether to use the services of a military placement firm. You just might have a few misconceptions about the whole process in the first place.

Let's debunk those misconceptions now by considering the following information graciously provided by Mr. Craig Griffin, SVP Operations of Bradley-Morris, Inc. (BMI), a leading military placement firm.

1. What are the benefits to using a military placement firm over conducting a self-search?

A military placement or recruiting firm should be able to fully prepare you for all aspects of the job search. This includes assisting you in preparing a professional resume and in educating you to the different types of jobs available in corporate America and the ability to match your skill set to the types of jobs that are a fit for you. Finally, you are provided thorough coaching for the entire interview process.

Military placement firms have deep relationships with companies from all over the world and are able to provide you with exposure. They are actively marketing the skills of military-experienced talent—your skills—to companies every day. The reputable firms are viewed as solution providers for clients who have the need and desire to acquire military talent.

The top firms should function as a personal advocate for you. Candidates should not feel as if they are being left to reside in a database wondering if a real person has ever even seen their resume after submitting it through a Web portal.

The sheer volume of opportunities that a leading military placement firm can expose a job seeker to will most likely dwarf what they could produce with only their own efforts. For example, BMI represents over 4,000 clients, and we have our finger on the pulse of their most current position needs, some that are not even being publicly advertised.

Finally, you should expect guidance through the entire process to help you accomplish the ultimate (and only) goal in the job search process: finding the job that you want. Accepting an offer for a job you are not really excited about is a surefire way to ensure you'll be repeating the whole job search process earlier than you would wish. Any agency worth its salt will work until both parties are sure they've found a good fit.

(continued)

(continued)

2. What should a job seeker understand about the working relationship between himself or herself and the placement firm?

First, ensure you choose a qualified firm that meets the following criteria:

- **Track record of success:** The firm should have multiple years in business, thousands of successful placements, and testimonials from candidates like you.

- **Free:** You should not have to pay anything for the job seeker service except potentially to travel to a hiring event or interview.

- **Nonexclusive:** You should be free to pursue your job search however you choose, including working with more than one military recruiting firm, as well as supplementing this activity with leveraging your personal network.

You should expect the agency representing you in your job search to be only as committed to the goal as you are. The job search is intense, and requires a firm commitment from the job seeker to be responsive, whether it's in the writing and revising of a resume or in the timely communication with both agency and client corporations. If you're not ready to commit the time necessary to complete the requirements and obligations of your job search, don't start.

Finally, understand the dynamic between the recruiting firm and its employer clients. Although the firm is motivated to place a candidate with the employer (the firm typically is paid only when a successful match is made), don't think that a reputable firm is looking to just put any warm body into a job. If the firm has any hope of winning repeat business, maintaining high client satisfaction, and advancing long-term client relationships, it is not in its interest to make bad matches.

Your salary is not being reduced in order for the employer to pay the recruiting firm. Understand that employers have different budgets for recruiting and for salaries.

- **The recruiting budget:** Employers use this budget to attract job seekers through employment advertising and job boards, to pay for employee referral programs, and to pay recruiting firms.

- **The employee compensation budget:** This includes salary, bonuses, and benefits. Your salary is commensurate with others in your position, with your experience, and in your city. Employees' compensation is not determined by how they were sourced, no matter if they applied on the company Web site, had their resume on a job board, or if they were found via a civilian or military recruiting firm.

3. What about the concept of exclusivity? Is it a good idea for a job seeker to agree to work with only one placement company at a time? Why or why not?

As I mentioned previously, an exclusive relationship with a military recruiting firm should be avoided at all costs. Exclusivity never benefits the job seeker. The only benefactor to an exclusive relationship is a placement agency that is not confident in either the number of opportunities it can present to you and/or the quality of opportunities that it can show you.

You want to give yourself as many options as possible. Applying for jobs with only one company or working exclusively with one transition resource is not in your best interests. Take advantage of all of the free services that are available (military placement firms, military job boards, military job fairs, TAP/ACAP, etc.) and that you have time to invest in.

4. Is there anything someone transitioning from the military can or should do prior to contacting a military placement firm to enhance chances for a successful placement?

I'm often questioned by military professionals who are several years out from their separation date about what "the best thing they can do to prepare themselves" might be as they finish out their military commitment. I've found the best answer is simply this: Perform to your absolute highest level in your current job. Companies in corporate America are always impressed by a

(continued)

(continued)

history of excellent performance. And whether through your military evaluations or the references that you provide to prospective employers, that performance will follow you throughout your entire career.

Don't be afraid to contact military firms far in advance of your transition (even if you haven't positively decided to transition out yet). We recommend at least two years in advance for JMOs (Junior Military Officers)/SMOs (Senior Military Officers) and six months in advance for NCOs (Non-Commissioned Officers)/ Enlisted. Reputable firms will record your proposed transition date and, if they have opportunities that match your background, will check back in with you to confirm your availability date and begin scheduling you for interviews.

Identify Your Work History, Marketable Skills, Abilities, and Experiences

Before you can persuade an employer to hire you, you have to have a clear understanding of what it is you have to offer him or her. Furthermore, you have to be able to express those marketable attributes verbally and in writing. This involves closely examining your past work history, your marketable skills and abilities, and your personal work values.

- **Your work history:** You may be able to recite your work history chapter and verse. Although that is admirable, writing it down in the form of a Master Career Catalog may be more beneficial at this point. Taking this step will help you lay the groundwork for developing your resume and provide you with detailed job application information for future use.

Master Career Catalog

Use this form to fully document your work history. Refer back to it as you develop your resume or as you complete job application forms.

I. Personal Information

Fill in the following information as applicable. Think of this as information that may appear on your resume.

Name: _____

Present address: _____

Future address: _____

Telephone: _____ E-mail: _____

II. Education and Training

List your academic education chronologically, beginning with the most recent. Include high school only if you graduated within the last five years.

College/university: _____

Dates attended: _____

Area of study: _____

Semester/credit hours completed: _____

Degree awarded (if applicable): _____

Remarks: _____

High school: _____

Dates attended: _____

Area of study: _____

Semester/credit hours completed: _____

Degree awarded (if applicable): _____

Remarks: _____

List your completed military training chronologically, beginning with the most recent. Make a note to indicate if you graduated a course with honors.

Course Title	Sponsor	Dates Attended
_____	_____	_____
_____	_____	_____

(continued)

(continued)

_____   _____   _____
_____   _____   _____
_____   _____   _____
_____   _____   _____
_____   _____   _____
_____   _____   _____
_____   _____   _____
_____   _____   _____
_____   _____   _____

III. Work Experience

Chart your work history for the last 10 years, beginning with your most recent position.

Job title: _____

Organization: _____

Address: _____

Dates: From _____ to _____

Supervisor: _____

Supervisor's telephone: _____

E-mail: _____

Beginning salary/pay grade: _____

Ending salary/pay grade: _____

Job responsibilities:

_____
_____
_____
_____
_____
_____

Job accomplishments:

_____
_____
_____
_____
_____
_____

IV. Potential References

Select individuals who can attest to your personal and professional integrity. Never use anyone's name without obtaining prior permission.

Name: _____ Job title: _____

Organization: _____

Telephone number: _____ E-mail: _____

Check all that apply:

Personal reference _____ Professional _____

Comments: _____

_____

_____

Name: _____ Job title: _____

Organization: _____

Telephone number: _____ E-mail: _____

Check all that apply:

Personal reference _____ Professional _____

Comments: _____

_____

_____

V. Other Relevant Information

Security clearance:

Yes: _____ Level: _____ No: _____

Foreign languages:

Computer skills (include software with which you are proficient):

_____

_____

Hobbies/interests: _____

Memberships: _____

Community involvement: _____

_____

Other information: _____

_____

_____

- **Your marketable skills and abilities:** After you have charted your career history, you will be able to better see where your talents lie. If doing so helps, go back through what you have completed in your work history and circle the main words that identify your skills and abilities. After you do that, carry this task one step further by classifying each one as a self-management skill, transferable skill, or dedicated skill. You might also think of other skills you did not include in your history. List them as well.

My Technical Skills

Technical skills are specific skills that are required to accomplish a given task. For example, if you are a network satellite engineer, you require network satellite engineering to accomplish your job.

_____

_____

_____

_____

_____

My Functional or Transferable Skills

Functional or transferable skills are common skills that may be used in different jobs and industries such as customer service, teaching, or consulting.

_____

_____

_____

_____

My Self-Management Skills

Self-management skills are skills that describe you as a person.
For example, you might be dependable and hard-working.

_____

_____

_____

_____

_____

_____

- **Personal work values and desires:** Your work history and your
  skills are important factors to consider as you plan for your
  next job. Equally important to consider are your personal
  work values. What matters to you? How do you want this next
  phase in your life to play out? Do you see yourself ramping up
  or powering down? Perhaps you've worked in a stressful job
  for a long time and want to avoid that in your next position.
  In the military, you're generally told what you're going to do
  and where you're going to do it. You have more of a choice as
  a civilian. That idea may be appealing to you, but it can also be
  overwhelming. Be kind to yourself and to your family. Carve
  out the time to examine what you want to achieve in this next
  life stage.

Something to Think About: Work Values That You May Already Value

Salary	Job Satisfaction	Praise
Job Success	Location	Flexibility
Work Schedule	Advancement	Benefits
Power	Status	Challenge
Security	Work Environment	Affiliation
Recognition	Service to Others	Independence

Something to Think About: Life Values That You May Already Value		
Health	Wealth	Family
Prestige	Job Satisfaction	Travel
Creativity	Freedom	Trust
Learning	Responsibility	Religion
Control	End Results	Respect
Intimacy	Friends	Honesty
Fun	Stability	Popularity
Affiliation	Recognition	Competition
Living Conditions	Culture	Progression

Identify Sources of Employment Opportunities

Potential sources of employment can be found anywhere. The job assistance resources mentioned earlier in this chapter provide information on job availability in addition to job search assistance. An extensive list of online resources is also provided to you in the appendix. You also should consider the following sources:

- **Hidden job market opportunities:** Networking is the way to find these opportunities. You will find out about more "hidden" job opportunities through casual conversation with well-connected friends and colleagues than you ever will by looking in the newspaper.

- **Job fairs:** If you attend a job fair, you may or may not walk away from it with an actual job. Chances are more the latter. What you will most certainly walk away with is information, and that is job search gold. Job fairs are a terrific place to meet people, gather business cards and company literature, and learn about real and projected opportunities. After the fair, your work begins in earnest. That is when you begin to tailor your resume to specific openings and write cover letters directly to individuals you met. Remember to track your activity!

- **Printed and online employment listings:** Job vacancies are advertised in printed form and in cyberspace in newspapers, trade journals, magazines, and on job boards. You won't have a problem finding job opportunities listed unless you are focusing your search on one tiny corner of the universe and refuse to look elsewhere. In this case, creativity might be a real requirement for your search. (See the appendix for more information regarding specific Web sites.)

- **Federal, state, and local offices:** According to the Department of Labor, there are more than 1.8 million civilian employees of the federal government, sans our federal postal employees. Clearly, the U.S. government is the nation's largest employer. Maybe there is a place for you in there somewhere. Federal employment opportunities may be located online at www.usajobs.gov. Contact your local state and city offices (or their respective Web sites) for potential employment opportunities, as well.

- **Industry directories:** Industry directories, available at your local library or online, can provide you with detailed information regarding a company's business, personnel, and financial stability.

- **Chambers of commerce:** Chambers are an excellent place to learn about businesses within the community. After all, their business is to attract business. Contact the chamber of commerce in the area you're interested in and inquire about a local employer listing. Usually, these lists, along with newcomer welcome packets, can be purchased at a minimal price.

Activate Your Network

Ours is a Facebook, MySpace, and LinkedIn world. Embrace it. Let those in your cyber reality know that you are actively seeking employment, but don't ignore those in your noncyber world while you're at it. Everyone you know should be aware that you are looking for employment. Word of mouth (or stroke of keyboard) is a productive tool in this process.

Networking is the act of developing and expanding your relationships with others. It is a continuous process that promotes a reciprocal exchange of information for the benefit of all parties. Your network is made stronger when you not only take from it, but also give back to it.

Tales from the Employed

Retire [or transition] from an area that you worked in while in the military so that you have made the necessary contacts. I retired on the East Coast and moved to a new town, so it was difficult to network for a job.

—*Laurie Davis, Independent Women's Health Care Consultant and U.S. Army Colonel (Ret.)*

The best jobs are found by networking. Sometimes a position will even be created for you!

—*Dale Michaels, Defense Contractor*

I was approached for a job by a couple of civilians that I had previously worked with at the flight line.

—*Thomas Wiederstein, Instructor, DOD Unmanned Aerial Vehicle (UAV) School*

You can see from the preceding comments, and you probably know from your own experience, that networking is key to the success of your job search. Take a few minutes and jot down the names of those you already know who could be of assistance to you. Think about your friends, neighbors, relatives, past and present coworkers and supervisors, and fellow members in any professional, personal, or religious organization.

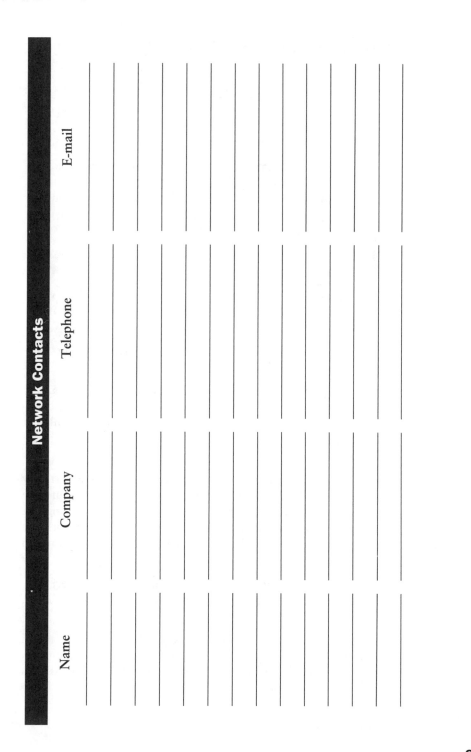

Network Contacts

Name	Company	Telephone	E-mail

Use Internet Job Boards Wisely

Before you begin posting your resume with wild abandon to every job board on the Internet, consider these valuable tips:

- Don't post your resume to every board you surf on. You're wasting your time and potentially an employer's time, and you're spreading your credentials too thin in the process.

- Use a localized search on reputable job boards such as Monster.com, Hotjobs.yahoo.com, Jobs.com, CareerBuilder. com, Careers.yahoo.com, and Net-Temps.com. Also consider targeting job boards that specialize in hiring those in your given career field.

- Never pay someone for the opportunity to post your resume to a particular site.

- Before you upload your resume, clearly understand how you can update it or withdraw it completely at a future date if you choose to do so.

- Take advantage of such online tools as job search agents provided by many of the sites.

- Understand that many jobs posted may not represent actual job openings but may instead be posted by recruiters, head-hunters, or executive search firms in an effort to accumulate a bank of resumes and potential candidates for future potential opportunities.

- Don't expect miracles or even responses. You most certainly aren't the only one posting your resume out there. One job opening could net thousands of resumes. You will distinguish yourself from the others by marrying the cyber you with the real you. In other words, get on the telephone for follow-up purposes.

- Make sure your resume is online-friendly (that is, convert your eye-appealing version to a text-only document sans bullets, elaborate fonts, and underlines).

- Remember that worlds will ultimately collide. If you maintain a wild and crazy persona online, it will eventually catch up to the professional you seeking a decent job. Mind your digital dirt and keep those cyberskeletons at bay!

Select Your References with Care

Employers often contact your references to ask them questions about you with regard to such areas as

- Length of employment.

- Quality of work performed.

- Level and scope of responsibility.

- Interpersonal skills.

- Timeliness (personal and professional).

- Reason for leaving previous employer.

- Potential disqualifications from future employment.

Make sure you choose and nurture your personal and professional references with care. You can have as many references as you like; however, having three to five is generally adequate. Before you use anyone's name, obtain permission to do so. Ask your references what they would say about you if called upon. Coach them if necessary. Network with these individuals, too. Keep them informed about your job search status. Avoid overuse of any one person's name. Don't include their names on your resume. Create a separate document that lists the following information for each reference:

- Name

- Company and job title

- Address

- Telephone and e-mail

- Relationship to you

Pitch Yourself

In your job search, you have to be able to confidently and intelligently talk about your skills, abilities, and qualifications. To this end, a two-minute sales pitch can be of great help and should contain the following:

- Relevant work experience

- Relevant skills or strengths

- Significant career accomplishments

- Applicable training or education

- A high-impact closing that clearly communicates your potential benefit to the company

You should prepare a short version and a longer version for use as the occasion demands. The goal here isn't to sound like a recording, however. Keep it natural and informative.

Be Realistic and Reasonable

You will have days when it seems as though everyone wants to hire you and days when you just want to give up. Don't throw in the towel when the going gets rough. Accept the fact that finding a job doesn't usually happen overnight. You may want to be employed your first day as a civilian, but reality says that doesn't always happen. The average job search can take anywhere from three to six months. If you focus too much on the future and not enough on the day-to-day requirements for getting to your goal, you will become quickly overwhelmed. Keep it real. Keep it in the present with the occasional thought splurge to the future. Manage your job search. Don't let events manage you.

CHAPTER 5

Writing Effective Resumes

Soon to be gone are the days when you can size up a person's basic qualifications by looking at the rank worn on his collar or the insignia on her uniform. Instead, you will need a resume.

A resume is a funny document. You can spend literally hours writing, editing, and rewriting it only to have a potential employer glance at it for a mere 20 seconds or less. Writing it hardly seems worth the effort given the eyeball to resume ratio, but write, edit, and rewrite you must.

Before you begin the excruciating process, you need to keep in mind several key concepts.

> **Key Concept #1: Your resume is written *about* you, not *for* you.**

You already have a high impression of yourself, don't you? Now it's time to make an impact on someone else who can give you a good job or lead you to one. Keep in mind that your resume should be targeted to the reader, not the writer.

After you've written your resume, you'll want to get a knowledgeable and objective second opinion (perhaps even a third) before you hand it out to anyone.

> **Key Concept #2: Your resume won't get you a job.**

As powerful as your resume may be, it won't land you a job all by its lonesome. If it is well written and if you have the required skills and experiences an employer is seeking, it may lead you to an interview where you can shine, sparkle, and finagle your way into employment, that being the intent of your resume in the first place.

Key Concept #3: There isn't just *one* correct way to write your resume.

To be sure, there are basic guidelines that the majority of job seekers follow and the majority of employers expect. Let your common sense, instinct, and research guide you as you go through this process. What works for others may not work for you. In our current state of high unemployment, even a judicious use of creativity can score you bonus points with the right employer.

Designing Your Resume Is as Easy as 1-2-3-4-5

You can always hire someone to write your resume for you. It's the easy, albeit expensive, way to go. (E-mail me if you have money to spend!) Keep in mind that when you have someone else pen your resume for you, you run the risk of losing your unique voice in the document. Never underestimate the power of your own voice. A highly skilled writer, who knows you well or has a good feel for your communication style, might be able to capture this quality in your resume, although this is generally not the case.

You can spare your wallet the pain of such a purchase and develop a resume that truly represents who you are professionally in skills, experiences, and voice. Here is a simple yet effective five-step plan for showcasing your hard-earned qualifications:

1. Identify the focus for your resume.

2. Identify the content and language for your resume.

3. Select the best format to use.

4. Identify additional experience and include as appropriate.

5. Review, edit, and revise your resume as necessary.

Step One: Identify the Focus for Your Resume

As you already know, employers typically give your resume a 20-second glance before they have subconsciously made their initial impression regarding it. Twenty seconds is not a lot of time to grab someone's attention, but it's what you must strive for anyway. Being concise, clear, and grammatically correct will help you to do just that. Your resume will stand a better chance if you clearly develop these three elements:

- The heading
- The objective
- The summary of your professional qualifications

Heading

The heading is usually the first thing the employer looks at on your resume. It tells him or her who you are and how you can be contacted. If it is presented the wrong way, it can also tell the employer more about you than you might want him or her to know right off the bat.

You should place your name on the first line of the resume (about one inch down from the top edge of the page), followed by your address, a telephone number or two, and an e-mail address. You don't need to add more than that. Avoid using your military rank or newly achieved "Retired" label anywhere in your heading.

Avoid: LTC Barbara Jones (Ret.)

Use: Barbara A. Jones

Exposing your rank right up front may backfire on you for two reasons. First, the civilian employer reading your resume may not have a clue what it means. Second, if the employer does understand what it means, he or she might interpret it as a point of self-inflated importance. Not to offend your sensibilities, but you're in a new world now. Sure, your rank may clue the employer into your requisite managerial level, but it may not impress him or her if he or she was in the military as well and held a lower rank, or likewise, if he or she has no clue of its meaning in the first place.

Also omit any reference to being a retiree, if that applies to you. A retiree in the military is not the same as a retiree in the civilian world, where this designation might conjure images of being a senior citizen. You don't need to suggest that at this point in your job search.

If you have an academic degree and it is a requirement for the job you're designing your resume for, tacking it on behind your name would be appropriate.

Use: James M. Michaels, M.Ed.

After your name, include your contact information. Sounds easy enough. As you well know, however, including an address can become a complicated issue when you are currently living in one place and transitioning to another.

For the ease of writing your resume, use your current mailing address. If you are stationed in one location and will be moving to another location and if you have an address where you can expect to receive mail, you may want to use a split heading. A split heading includes two addresses. For example:

John M. Michaels
john.michaels@myemail.com

Present:
525 Catalina Drive
Sierra Vista, Arizona 00000
(555) 555-5555

After July 1:
1414 Main Street
Tampa, Florida 00000
(555) 555-5555

Notice a couple of issues here. First, the name is bolded and uses a slightly larger font size than the e-mail address beneath it. By doing this, you place more emphasis on your name, which is what you're trying to get the employer to remember. In this example, the e-mail address is placed directly underneath the name, in a font that is one point smaller and italicized. The nice thing about your name and e-mail is that both of them stay the same, regardless of where you are physically located.

Whether or not you use a split heading approach will, of course, depend on your immediate travel plans. If you are planning to stay in the same area, your heading could follow this format:

John M. Michaels
525 Catalina Drive
Sierra Vista, Arizona 00000
(555) 555-5555
john.michaels@myemail.com

The name is still boldfaced and typed in a larger font, giving it emphasis. The address and e-mail follow, centered under the name.

If your resume is more than one page in length, you do not need to repeat the entire heading on the second page. Include your bolded name and indicate that it is page two. For example:

John M. Michaels   Page Two

or

John M. Michaels
Page Two

Remember, these are just examples of formatting. There are multiple ways that you can illustrate this information. The key is to strive for a professional appearance. Yet another cliché lives on: You don't get a second chance to make a first impression.

Objective

Your resume should have a unifying theme, supported by each and every word on it. You are the topic. Your skills, experience, and talents are the guts of it. Strive to write in such a way that you appear to know what you want to do, whether or not that's actually the case.

Resume writing experts continue to argue whether you need to include an objective statement on your resume. One can easily make a case for or against the practice; however, one fact is clear: Your resume must have an implied objective, whether or not it is physically written outright. Without an objective, you lack focus. Without focus, you flounder. Every line on your resume should support your stated or unstated objective. If it doesn't, you should question whether that line belongs on your resume at all. **The objective is that important.**

If you want to stay in your present career field, coming up with an objective shouldn't be difficult. You can make it broad-based toward an industry or zoom in on a specific job with a specific company. For example:

> **Broad-based objective:** A managerial position within the telecommunications industry.

> **Specific objective:** Director of Operations for Your Great Company, Inc.

If you want to switch career fields, you need to be creative in writing your objective, depending on your actual exposure to and experience in that desired field. If you're switching gears drastically, you'll need to make a concerted effort to market your transferable skills.

By including your objective on your resume, you give the employer a break by defining your wishes immediately. Employers like that. This is a good use of your 20 seconds.

Don't include an objective if you're creating a resume for use in a job fair, where there may be multiple opportunities to consider, or if you're passing off your resume to a contact at a company that doesn't have a specific opening announced.

A clearly written objective can do wonders for your chances of obtaining an interview. Each time you apply for a different job, you need to be certain that your objective (whether or not you include it on your resume) matches the position for which you are applying.

Summary of Your Professional Qualifications

Like the job objective, a summary of qualifications section can help your resume survive that initial scanning process. It gives the employer a quick synopsis of your experience and specialized expertise. It immediately shows him or her whether there is potential for a match between you and the job. Your summary should contain big-picture (yet targeted and relevant) information as it directly relates to the job you're applying for. Specifically, it might contain

- The number of years of experience you have in your field

- Any specialized expertise or required credentials you may have, such as a top-secret security clearance

- Mention of your more outstanding management skills or technical abilities

Here is a sample summary for a resume targeted toward law enforcement:

```
Ten years of experience in the field of law enforcement
with emphasis on management, crime prevention, criminal
investigations, and patrol. Knowledgeable of federal,
state, and local laws and ordinances. Excellent
communication and investigative skills. Computer
literate. Weapons qualified. Maintain Department of
Defense secret security clearance. Physically fit. Drug
free. Recognized on a number of occasions for superior
police work under stressful circumstances.
```

Here is the same summary shown in a different layout:

- Ten years of law enforcement experience with emphasis on management, crime prevention, criminal investigations, and patrol.

- Knowledgeable of federal, state, and local laws and ordinances.

- Excellent communication and investigative skills.

- Computer literate.

- Weapons qualified.

- Maintain Department of Defense secret security clearance.

- Physically fit and drug free.

- Recognized on a number of occasions for superior police work under stressful circumstances.

Your summary should be just that: a summary. It should not take up half the page. Each time you apply for a different job, you should tailor this summary to the important skills sought by the employer for the job. Doing this takes some effort, but details count. Attention to detail will determine whether you get a job interview.

Step Two: Identify the Content and Language for Your Resume

No doubt you have a lot of experience from which you can draw; however, you can't include all of it in one resume. If you have a number of years of experience, deciding what to include and what to omit can be difficult. The key is to focus on what is *most relevant*.

If it helps you to focus, ask yourself this question:

> Does this experience fully support my job objective for this resume?

For example, does your future employer really need to know you graduated with honors from the exclusive military action officer's writing course? Probably not. If, on the other hand, the answer is yes, include this fact.

Be forewarned. You will have countless experiences that you won't include on your resume. That's okay. Accept that fact, and whatever you do, avoid changing to 3-point type so that you can squish it all in. You'll look far too desperate if you go that route.

Using the Right Lingo

In addition to deciding the content for your resume, you have to decide what type of language to use—military jargon or everyday English.

If you're targeting a job within the defense industry, feel free to use the military jargon, within reason, to which you've become accustomed. The defense industry likes to hire employees who understand the lingo.

On the other hand, if you're targeting a job outside that arena, you may have to use everyday English specific to the industry. If you were to take someone who has never been exposed to life in the military and plant him or her in the middle of a typical conversation between service members discussing work, that person would probably feel like a stranger in an even stranger land.

The military loves its acronyms. When you get used to them, they're not so bad; however, civilian employers may not understand them at all. The following translations may assist you in crafting your resume and your speech. Note that some words or job titles may be clearly understood without changing them at all.

Common Translations

In the Military	In the Civilian World
Commander	Director/Senior Manager/President
Executive Officer	Deputy Director/Assistant
Action Officer	Senior Analyst
Branch or Division Chief	Branch/Division Chief
Program or Project Manager	Program or Project Manager
General officer	President/Senior Director Chairperson
	Chief Executive Officer (CEO)
	Chief Operating Officer (COO)

In the Military	In the Civilian World
	Chief Financial Officer (CFO)
	Senior Vice President
	Executive Vice President
Senior field grade officer	Senior Administrator/Chief Executive
	Department head/Program Director
	Deputy Chief/Senior Executive
Field grade officer	Executive/Manager
Company grade officer	Associate/Operations Officer
	Unit or Section Manager
Warrant officer	Director/Specialist/Department Manager
Senior NCO	Director/First-Line Supervisor
Infantry	Ground security force
Sergeant Major	Senior Advisor
First Sergeant	Personnel Manager
Squad Leader	Team Leader/Team Chief
Supply Sergeant	Supply Manager/Logistics Manager
Operations NCO	Operations Manager
NCO	Supervisor/Manager
OER/NCOER	performance rating/evaluation
AI	additionally skilled in...
AAM-ARCOM	award/recognition
ANCOC/BNCOC	advanced (specialty) course
battalion (BN)	unit/organization/agency

(continued)

(continued)

In the Military	In the Civilian World
headquarters	headquarters
combat	conflict/hostilities/emergency
	highly hazardous conditions
garrison	organization/company
company	company/unit/department
correspondence course	extension course/distance learning
	correspondence course
leader	supervisor/manager
medal	award/recognition
military personnel office (MILPO)	personnel office
mission	task/function/objective
military occupation specialty (MOS)	career specialty
platoon	section/element/department
Platoon Sergeant	Supervisor/Instructor/Trainer
physical training (PT)	physical training
reconnaissance	data collection/survey/analysis
regulations	policy/guidelines/instructions
security clearance	security clearance
soldiers/airmen/marines/ sailors	personnel/staff/employees/ individuals/people
subordinates	employees/personnel/staff/ individuals/people
Temporary Duty (TDY)	business trip/temporary duty
Uniform Code of Military Justice (UCMJ)	legal action/document

In the Military	In the Civilian World
TDA/MTOE	organizational structure/human and material resources
Personnel Action Center (PAC)	personnel office
AR/DA/NAV Pamphlets	policy/guidelines/rules
team	team
squad	section
brigade	group/division
battalion	division
PLDC/BNCOC	leadership or advanced leadership development course
Command and General Staff College	Strategic Management Course
War College	Advanced Strategic Studies Course
Area of Operations (AOR)	venue/organization/realm of responsibility
QA/QC	QA/QC (but spell it out the first time!)

It's important to write your resume in the language of the industry you are targeting. To help you better translate what you've done in the military into language that is easily understood by someone not familiar with the jargon, consult the O*NET OnLine Web site at the following address:

http://online.onetcenter.org

The O*NET is an extensive database of worker attributes and characteristics. It is also a great tool that can help you capture the civilian essence of your ever-so-military job by using a crosswalk feature.

The unique military-to-civilian crosswalk feature not only provides you with a civilian job title and description equivalent, however. It also leads you to report options offering you more information than you ever wanted to know about the field itself and links to specific state wages and employment information, compliments of CareerInfoNet.

After you read the job description, don't be tempted to copy it verbatim onto your resume. Instead, read and analyze it for applicability in your own case. For example, notice the keywords that appear. Do those same keywords apply to your experience? What about the knowledges, skills, and abilities (KSAs)? Do any of them ring a bell in your camouflaged history? Maybe you called something by a different name in the military, but the basic job function itself is the same. Make the connections with your inner civilian.

Resume Sentence Structure

Resume sentences are not real sentences. They are fragments, and using them for this purpose is perfectly acceptable.

When you write sentence fragments, you omit the subject—in this case, you.

> **Don't Use:** I managed a staff of 45 analysts.

> **Use:** Managed staff of 45 analysts.

Additionally, your statements should be accomplishment-based and should not read like an evaluation report or job description.

Finally, your sentences should aim to quantify your accomplishments, making your credentials more action-based. Consider the following two examples:

> **Example 1:** Managed a personnel division.

> **Example 2:** Effectively managed 100+-employee-strong manpower and personnel division that provided services for Department of Defense employees throughout Europe.

Obviously, Example 2 gives more detail without going overboard. Here are several other examples:

- Successfully increased output by 35 percent in less than two months.

- Supervised development and implementation of self-directed training module.

- Effectively and efficiently managed staff of 50 technicians working in 24-hour telecommunications facility.

To get the attention of potential employers, your resume must contain words that communicate action. The following list of power words may help you to think of those that apply to your experiences:

Accounted	Acted	Adapted
Administered	Analyzed	Assessed
Budgeted	Built	Calculated
Classified	Coached	Compared
Conceptualized	Conducted	Consolidated
Consulted	Coordinated	Counseled
Created	Defined	Delegated
Designed	Developed	Directed
Edited	Eliminated	Established
Examined	Expanded	Facilitated
Generated	Guided	Headed
Identified	Implemented	Improved
Instructed	Investigated	Led
Maintained	Managed	Marketed
Mentored	Merged	Negotiated
Obtained	Operated	Organized
Performed	Planned	Presented
Projected	Provided	Published
Recognized	Recommended	Recorded
Reorganized	Repaired	Researched
Scheduled	Shaped	Simplified
Standardized	Streamlined	Synthesized
Trained	Troubleshot	Unified
Upgraded	Validated	Worked
Wrote		

Step Three: Select the Best Format to Use

After you have decided which skills and experiences to highlight and which can be omitted, you must select a resume format. We will discuss these formats in depth:

- Chronological resumes
- Combination resumes
- Contract resumes
- Curriculum vitae (CVs)
- Federal resumes

Chronological Resumes

The tried-and-true chronological resume is the format most employers prefer to see. This simple format lays out your qualifications in a timeline fashion, beginning with your most recent experience and working backward. This resume format is best used if you have a proven track record in a specific career field and wish to remain in that field. In such a case, your resume is likely to illustrate career progression, and that is a certainly a plus. This format also works with recent high school or college graduates.

Take a look at the two sample chronological resumes, one labeled "before" (Figure 5.1) and the other "after" (Figure 5.2). In both resumes, the format clearly illustrates the candidate's contact information, general background, specific experience, and education. The "before" resume is clearly a decent first draft of a chronological resume. Let's look at it more closely, comparing it to the "after" version so you can get a feel for the difference between a good resume and a great resume.

David Masters
HHC 00th, APO AE 55555
011-974-555-5555
david.masters@myemail.com

OBJECTIVE: Seeking a position as a Maintenance Supervisor.

SUMMARY OF QUALIFICATIONS

• More than 24 years of military experience, including 10 years as a Maintenance Supervisor.
• Granted a Secret Clearance by the U.S. Government, active until 2017.
• Possess outstanding organizational and time management skills.
• Able to operate heavy- and light-wheeled vehicles, forklifts, and power generation equipment.
• Monitored production, quality control, and work flow as a maintenance/operations supervisor.
• Oversaw programs in safety, calibration, QAJQC, AOAP, driver training, and physical fitness.
• Diagnosed malfunctions; performed and supervised corrective maintenance on diesel engines and power-generating units, including accessories, power trains, and chassis components of wheeled vehicles.
• Proficient in Microsoft Office.

EMPLOYMENT HISTORY

QA/QC, March 2008 – Present, AMC/QA, U.S. Army, Doha, Qatar

• Provide technical guidance and/or advice to the Contractors' technical staff, clarifying Government drawings, specifications designs, statements of work, and performance requirements within defined limitations.
• Provide production plans for the unit's AFSB, APS-5 equipment; enforce quality assurance plans, policies, procedures, and standards.
• Review reports on costs incurred, as requested, to determine that quality and quantity of the materials and service are in accordance with the Contractor.
• Provide the ACO a monthly activity report; notify the Contractor of deficiencies observed during surveillance.

Motor Sergeant, January 2007–March 2008 U.S. Army, Fort Benning, GA

• Provided technical guidance to subordinates; diagnosed automotive system faults at all levels of maintenance.
• Performed equipment inspections, quality assurance /quality control (QA, QC), automated repair parts procedures, Army Oil Analysis Program (AOAP), calibration, key control, and coordination with units and activities.
• Responsible for maintenance and recovery operations on 257 tactical vehicles; supervised and provided technical guidance to 25 soldiers.

Motor Sergeant, June 2005– December 2006 U.S. Army, Fort Lewis, WA

• Supervised, planned, and directed Battalion Level Maintenance; diagnosed malfunctions; performed and supervised corrective maintenance on diesel engines and power-generating units.
• Performed equipment inspections and quality assurance/quality control (QA, QC) on three Companies within my area of operations (AOR).

Figure 5.1: Sample chronological resume before improvements.   *(continued)*

(continued)

David Masters
HHC 00th, APO AE 55555
011-974-555-5555
david.masters@myemail.com
Page 2

• Responsible for maintenance and recovery operations on 300 tactical vehicles and 128 ancillary pieces of equipment; also provided support to the units within my AOR.
• Supervised and provided technical guidance to 20 maintenance personnel and four logistics clerks.
• Developed and executed company drivers training program and maintenance inspection procedures for the division alert-holding area.

Senior Maintenance Supervisor, July 2002 – May 2005, U.S. Army, Vilseck, Germany

• Provided guidance and oversight to unit maintenance control sergeants in shop operations, calibrations, and parts requisitions.
• Revised brigade calibration program during Garrison operations and managed brigade Army oil analysis program during National Training Center rotation.
• Developed and executed unit drivers training program.
• Performed organizational and direct support maintenance on both light- and heavy-wheeled vehicles.
• Repaired deficiencies and shortcomings detected during equipment operation and performance of services.
• Repaired power-assisted brake systems, wheeled-vehicle suspension, steering, and electrical systems, compression ignition engines, and transmission assemblies.
• Ensured maintenance personnel had proper qualifications and were properly trained and motivated to work productively, both as part of a team and as individuals utilizing all TPM processes.

Senior Heavy-Wheeled, Vehicle Mechanic, Feb 2000 - May 2002, US Army, Fort Irwin, CA

• Performed organizational and direct support maintenance on both light- and heavy-wheeled vehicles.
• Repaired deficiencies and shortcomings detected during equipment operation and performance of services.
• Repaired power-assisted brake systems, wheeled-vehicle suspension, steering, and electrical systems, compression ignition engines, and transmission assemblies.

CERTIFICATION/EDUCATION/TRAINING

- Clearance: Secret Clearance active until 2017
- Civilian Education: Austin Peay University, A.A., Business Management, Clarksville, TN, 2003 Northwest High School, Clarksville, TN, 1984

Military Schooling:
- DOD Government Purchase Card. ClG 00 I, 2008
- Contract Format and Structure for DOD, ClC 033, 2008
- Acquisition Reporting Concepts and Policy, CLB 014. 2008
- Contracting Officers Representative Overview, CLC 012. 2008

David Masters
HHC 00th, APO AE 55555
011-974-555-5555
david.masters@myemail.com
Page 3

- Contract Terminations, ClC 006. 2008
- Acquisition Logistics Fundamentals, LOG 10 L 2008
- Advanced Noncommissioned Officer Course (ANCOC), 2005
- Automated Air Load Planning System (U MO 153), 2003
- Unit Movement Officer (UMO 151). 2003
- Airlift Planner's Course (UMO 152),2003
- Basic Noncommissioned Officer Course (BNCOC), 2001
- Heavy-Wheeled Vehicle Mechanic. 1999-2000
- Joint Personal Property Course, 1999
- Primary Leadership Development Course (PLDC), 1989
- Hawk Launcher and Mechanical System Repairer, 1988
- Personal Finance, 1986
- Traffic Management Coordination, 1985

David Masters
HHC 00th, APO AE 55555
011-974-555-5555
david.masters@myemail.com

OBJECTIVE
Seeking a position as a maintenance supervisor.

SUMMARY OF QUALIFICATIONS
More than 24 years of work experience with emphasis on maintenance supervision. Effectively monitored production, quality control, and work flow of operations. Oversaw safety, calibration, and oil analysis programs. Diagnosed malfunctions and supervised the corrective maintenance on diesel engines and power-generating units including accessories, power trains, and chassis components of wheeled vehicles. Maintain a current secret security clearance. Outstanding organizational and time management skills. Skilled in operating heavy- and light-wheeled vehicles, forklifts, and power generation equipment. Computer literate. Proficient using MS Office. Willing to relocate and work flexible shifts.

EMPLOYMENT HISTORY

Quality Assurance/Control (QA/QC) Supervisor
AMC/QA, U.S. Army, Doha, Qatar, 2008–Present

- Provide guidance and advice to the contractors' technical staff, clarifying government drawings, specification designs, statements of work, and performance requirements.
- Provide and enforce unit quality assurance plans, policies, procedures, and standards.
- Review reports on costs incurred to ensure contractor compliance.
- Create and furnish the contract lead with a monthly activity report noting any deficiencies.

Motor Operations Supervisor
U.S. Army, Fort Benning, GA, 2007–2008

- Provided guidance to 25 technicians, helping them to diagnose automotive system faults at all levels of maintenance.
- Performed equipment inspections, QA/QC, automated repair parts procedures, Army Oil Analysis Program (AOAP), calibration, key control, and coordination with units and activities.
- Responsible for maintenance and recovery operations on 257 tactical vehicles.

Motor Operations Supervisor
U.S. Army, Fort Lewis, WA, 2005–2006

- Supervised, planned, and directed 24 personnel performing higher-level maintenance activities.
- Diagnosed malfunctions and performed or supervised corrective maintenance on diesel engines and power-generating units.
- Performed equipment inspections and QA/QC for three large departments within the organization.
- Maintained and performed recovery operations on 300 tactical vehicles and 128 ancillary pieces of equipment.
- Developed and implemented company drivers training program and maintenance inspection procedures for the organization.

Figure 5.2: Sample chronological resume after improvements.

David Masters
Page Two

Senior Maintenance Supervisor
U.S. Army, Vilseck, Germany, 2002–2005

- Provided guidance to unit maintenance control supervisors in regards to shop operations, calibrations, and parts requisitions.
- Revised organizational calibration program and managed the oil analysis program.
- Developed and implemented a highly effective unit drivers training program.
- Performed direct support maintenance on both light- and heavy-wheeled vehicles.
- Repaired deficiencies and shortcomings detected during equipment operation and performance of services.
- Repaired power-assisted brake systems; wheeled-vehicle suspension, steering, and electrical systems; compression ignition engines; and transmission assemblies.
- Ensured maintenance personnel were qualified and properly trained to work productively, both as part of a team and as individuals utilizing all organizational processes.

Senior Heavy-Wheeled Vehicle Mechanic
U.S. Army, Fort Irwin, CA, 2000–2002

- Performed maintenance on both light- and heavy-wheeled vehicles, repairing deficiencies.
- Repaired power-assisted brake systems; wheeled-vehicle suspension, steering, and electrical systems; compression ignition engines; and transmission assemblies.

EDUCATION AND TRAINING

- Associate's Degree, Business Management, Austin Peay University, 2003
- Department of Defense Contract Format and Structure Course, U.S. Army, 2008
- Acquisition Reporting Concepts and Policy Course, U.S. Army, 2008
- Contracting Officers Representative Overview, U.S. Army, 2008
- Contract Terminations Training, U.S. Army, 2008
- Acquisition Logistics Fundamentals Course, U.S. Army, 2008
- Advanced Leadership Course, U.S. Army, 2005
- Automated Air Load Planning System Course, U.S. Army, 2003
- Unit Movement Officer Course, U.S. Army, 2003
- Airlift Planner's Course, U.S. Army, 2003

The Heading

Before: The heading is listed on three pages. This is unnecessary. Also, a three-page chronological resume is far too long for this format. The content for the heading on page one is appropriate, however.

After: The heading is positioned once on the first page, while only the name and page number, bolded for emphasis, appear on page two. Notice page three is gone, and the name is bolded and a font size bigger than the address, putting more attention on the name of the job seeker.

The Objective

Before: The positioning of the objective doesn't stand out from the resume, making everything seem to run together. Not very eye-friendly. As far as the content, the objective itself is somewhat vague. Until the job seeker applies for a specific position, this will do, however.

After: With the word *Objective* centered and the text underneath it centered as well, this section now grabs the reader's attention a bit more. Remember that 20 seconds of sell time! Capitalize on it.

The Summary of Qualifications

Before: This version has gone a little bullet crazy. Of course, using bullets in your resume is good when you know for certain it is not going to be scanned and read by a computer. They draw attention to specific lines; however, overusing them detracts from the overall readability.

The content itself in the summary gets a bit too detailed here.

After: To eliminate the overuse of bullets, I reformatted the summary of qualifications in this version into a paragraph form.

The content here has been streamlined somewhat. The detail regarding the security clearance has been eliminated, and the random acts of capitalization have been deleted.

The important information, previously buried in the summary, has been brought forward and shortened, with emphasis being placed on the supervisory aspect rather than the operator aspect.

Here, the computer skills line has been expanded somewhat with the assumption that there is more going for the job seeker than just MS Office.

And finally, an extra note has been added about the job seeker's willingness to relocate for the job and to work flexible shifts, with the assumption that this is true.

As the job seeker applies for different positions, he can go back in and add or subtract relevant content to best match his credentials to the opportunity at hand.

The Employment History

Before: The experience blocks are well done for a first draft. The resume suffers, however, from some degree of abuse in terms of random acts of capitalization and overuse of the semicolon (which, by the way, is generally a dead giveaway to content copied from another source).

Although efforts have clearly been made to identify some of the acronyms, some are identified after being used previously, and there are just too many, particularly if the job seeker is targeting a civilian company versus a defense contractor.

After: In this version, the job experience blocks have been edited significantly. Job titles have been bolded, and employers, locations, and dates italicized and not bolded, putting more attention on the job title. Translations have been provided for the civilian mindset, and the whole section itself has been shortened. Personal pronouns and repetitive statements have been deleted.

Compare the two and see whether you agree that the "after" version appears more marketable.

The Education Section

Before: This section contains way too much information, some of it not even relevant to the objective (at least on the surface without knowing more about the job it is being applied against).

After: A complete rewrite of this section has occurred and not a moment too soon. The distinction between civilian education and military schooling has been deleted, and the security clearance reference has been erased because it is already provided within the summary on page one.

A number of entries, some too old or not relevant, have been left off in this version. For example, high school, Basic Non-Commissioned Officer's Course (BNOC), and personal finance courses have been deleted, among others.

General Comments

Again, the "before" resume isn't a bad one. It is a good first draft. With a little tweaking here and tailoring there, you can easily end up with an "after" version sure to grab an employer's attention.

Combination Resumes

Sometimes the comfortable chronological format just doesn't cut it. Suppose you don't want to stay on your present career path. You want to do something different. Or perhaps you want to stay in your field but want to highlight specific skills and talents that may be buried in the timeline of a chronological format.

Enter the combination resume format for your marketing pleasure. The combination resume combines the chronological resume with what is known as a functional resume. Let's discuss the difference between the two for clarity's sake.

A functional resume primarily highlights your skill areas and education versus your chronological work history. It usually does not reflect your work history, which is a critical factor to potential employers. (A purely functional resume would be more appropriate for a high school or college graduate who hasn't had any work experience at all.)

The combination resume, on the other hand, combines the strengths of both formats. It not only highlights your skills, abilities, and training, but also provides the employer with the all-important work history in the chronological format. This highly adaptable resume can be used in a number of situations and is therefore discussed here in lieu of the purely functional format.

Figure 5.3 shows the chronological resume used earlier, organized in a combination format. As you can see, the combination format nicely groups areas of expertise into summarizing paragraphs. It allows the employer to get a total feel for the applicant's depth of experience in one area versus trying to piece together all instances of experience throughout a given time period.

David Masters
HHC 00th, APO AE 55555
011-974-555-5555
david.masters@myemail.com

OBJECTIVE
Seeking a position as a maintenance supervisor.

SUMMARY OF QUALIFICATIONS
More than 24 years of work experience with emphasis on maintenance supervision, quality assurance (QA), quality control (QC), and operations. Effectively monitored production, quality control, and work flow of operations. Oversaw safety, calibration, and oil analysis programs. Diagnosed malfunctions and supervised the corrective maintenance on diesel engines and power-generating units, including accessories, power trains, and chassis components of wheeled vehicles. Maintain a current secret security clearance. Outstanding organizational and time management skills. Skilled in operating heavy- and light-wheeled vehicles, forklifts, and power generation equipment. Computer literate. Proficient using MS Office. Willing to relocate and work flexible shifts.

AREAS OF EXPERTISE

Maintenance Supervision
Supervised, planned, and directed over 50 personnel performing higher-level maintenance activities. Assisted technicians in diagnosing automotive system faults at all levels of maintenance. Ensured that maintenance and recovery operations on 257 tactical vehicles were conducted on schedule. Provided guidance to unit maintenance control supervisors in regards to shop operations, calibrations, and parts requisitions. Ensured maintenance employees were qualified and properly trained to work productively, both as part of a team and as individuals utilizing all organizational processes. Developed and implemented company drivers training program and maintenance inspection procedures for the organization.

Quality Assurance and Control
Performed equipment inspections, QA/QC, automated repair parts procedures, Army Oil Analysis Program (AOAP), calibration, key control, and coordination with numerous units and activities. Revised organizational calibration program and managed the oil analysis program. Reviewed reports on costs incurred to ensure contractor compliance. Created and furnished the contractor lead with a monthly activity report noting any deficiencies. Provided and enforced unit quality assurance plans, policies, procedures, and standards. Provided guidance and advice to the contractors' technical staff, clarifying government drawings, specification designs, statements of work, and performance requirements.

Maintenance Operations
Maintained and performed recovery operations on 300 tactical vehicles and 128 ancillary pieces of equipment. Diagnosed malfunctions and performed corrective maintenance on diesel engines and power-generating units. Performed direct support maintenance on both light- and heavy-wheeled vehicles. Repaired power-assisted brake systems; wheeled-vehicle suspension, steering, and electrical systems; compression ignition engines; and transmission assemblies.

Figure 5.3: Sample combination resume.

(continued)

(continued)

David Masters
Page Two

EDUCATON AND TRAINING
- Associate's Degree, Business Management, Austin Peay University, 2003
- Department of Defense Contract Format and Structure Course, U.S. Army, 2008
- Acquisition Reporting Concepts and Policy Course, U.S. Army, 2008
- Contracting Officers Representative Overview, U.S. Army, 2008
- Contract Terminations Training, U.S. Army, 2008
- Acquisition Logistics Fundamentals Course, U.S. Army, 2008
- Advanced Leadership Course, U.S. Army, 2005
- Automated Air Load Planning System Course, U.S. Army, 2003
- Unit Movement Officer Course, U.S. Army, 2003
- Airlift Planner's Course, U.S. Army, 2003

WORK HISTORY
Quality Assurance/Control (QA/QC) Supervisor
AMC/QA, U.S. Army, Doha, Qatar, 2008–Present

Motor Operations Supervisor
U.S. Army, Fort Benning, GA, 2007–2008

Motor Operations Supervisor
U.S. Army, Fort Lewis, WA, 2005–2006

Senior Maintenance Supervisor
U.S. Army, Vilseck, Germany, 2002–2005

Senior Heavy-Wheeled Vehicle Mechanic
U.S. Army, Fort Irwin, CA, 2000–2002

To create the combination format, you have to first identify your skill headings ("Areas of Expertise" on this example). Then you have to go back and fill in the blanks, so to speak. As you do this, you pull from across your career, not limiting yourself to a timeline. Instead, you pick and choose the experiences that best support your heading and your overall objective.

The heading, objective, summary, and education blocks are the same. Only in the work experience/history areas do we adjust fire here.

Sample Combination Skill Headings

In the process of developing a combination resume, you will need to clearly label your areas of expertise. If you are targeting a specific career field, this task should be easy. Don't neglect other areas that may support your job objective, however. The following lists provide you with ideas for identifying your areas of expertise.

Area: Management, Supervision, and Administration

Management	Supervision	Administration
Quality Assurance	Logistics	Coordination
Professional Support	Program Management	Conflict Resolution
Problem Solving	Staff Development	Statistical Analysis
Program Analysis		

Area: Communications, Information Management

Network Engineering	Information Management	Equipment Maintenance
Systems Analysis	Telecommunications	Computer Security
Satellite Control	Communications	Customer Service
Technical Support	Information Analysis	

Area: Office Administration

Scheduling	Office Automation	Customer Relations
Accounts Management	Correspondence	Office Administration
Data Entry		

Area: Sales and Training

Market Research	Customer Relations	Purchasing
Product Knowledge	Program Development	Curriculum Evaluation
Testing	Training	Sales Management
Advertising	Market Analysis	

Area: Technical, Mechanical, and Construction

Schematics	Assembly	Diagnostics
Projects	Calibration	Transportation
Technical Knowledge	Installation and Maintenance	

Area: Transportation/Logistics

Driving	Instruction	Vehicle Operations
Transportation	Hazardous Materials	Environmental Safety
Safety	Quality Control	Supply Management
Property Accountability	Shipping and Receiving	Inventory Management
Customer Service		

Area: Food Service

Menu Planning	Nutrition	Catering
Food Storage	Food Preparation	Facility Management
Customer Service		

Contract Resumes

Contract resumes defy all commonly accepted laws of resume writing. Accept that fact up front. A contract resume easily can run up to 20 pages. It has a different purpose than your ordinary, run-of-the-mill resume.

Many prior military service members choose to work as civilians in the defense industry. The way a contract resume usually works is that you create your "ordinary" resume and submit it to a contractor. (Note: If you are well known already to such contractors, they will probably forgo this step and ask you for the contract version of your resume right away.) If your qualifications are well received along the way, you will probably be asked to revise your resume in a much more detailed fashion. This revision generally turns out to be a total rewrite of your resume in far more excruciating detail than you ever imagined.

If you want to work for contractors like this, you must abide by their wishes. Their intent is not to torment you. They must show management, in explicit detail, how your qualifications match the exact requirements for a position working on a particular contract. In essence, your resume becomes a technical part of their contract and must adhere to a specific format.

As you can see in Figure 5.4, the contract resume is the mother of all resumes. It ignores conventional resume wisdom, and that is acceptable in such situations. Remember, the right resume format to use is the one that the employer wants to see in the first place.

DAVID MASTERS
HHC 00th, APO AE 55555 • 011-974-555-5555 • david.masters@myemail.com

SUMMARY OF QUALIFICATIONS:

Maintenance Supervision	Heavy- and Light-Wheeled Vehicles
Operation and Production	Power Generation Equipment
Quality Control	Diesel Engine Maintenance
Work Flow Analysis	Personnel Management
Safety Programs	Calibration and Oil Analysis
Forklift Operations	Microsoft Office Products

WORK EXPERIENCE:

Quality Assurance/Control (QA/QC) Supervisor
December 2008–Present, AMC/QA, U.S. Army, Doha, Qatar

Duties/Responsibilities:
Provide guidance and advice to the contractors' technical staff, clarifying government drawings, specification designs, statements of work, and performance requirements. Provide and enforce unit quality assurance plans, policies, procedures, and standards. Review reports on costs incurred to ensure contractor compliance. Create and furnish the contract lead with a monthly activity report noting any deficiencies.

Motor Operations Supervisor
May 2007–December 2008, U.S. Army, 192nd Infantry Brigade, Fort Benning, Georgia

Duties/Responsibilities:
Guided 25 technicians, helping them to diagnose automotive system faults at all levels of maintenance. Performed equipment inspections, QA/QC, automated repair parts procedures, Army Oil Analysis Program (AOAP), calibration, key control, and coordination with units and activities. Responsible for maintenance and recovery operations on 257 tactical vehicles.

Motor Operations Supervisor
January 2005–May 2007, U.S. Army, 25th Infantry Division, Fort Lewis, Washington

Duties/Responsibilities:
Supervised, planned, and directed 24 personnel performing higher-level maintenance activities. Diagnosed malfunctions and performed or supervised corrective maintenance on diesel engines and power-generating units. Performed equipment inspections and QA/QC for three large departments within the organization. Maintained and performed recovery operations on 300 tactical vehicles and 128 ancillary pieces of equipment. Developed and implemented company drivers training program and maintenance inspection procedures for the organization.

Figure 5.4: Sample contract resume.

DAVID MASTERS, Page Two

Senior Maintenance Supervisor
July 2002–January 2005, U.S. Army, 409th Base Support Battalion, Vilseck, Germany

Duties/Responsibilities:
Guided unit maintenance control supervisors in regards to shop operations, calibrations, and parts requisitions. Revised organizational calibration program and managed the oil analysis program. Developed and implemented a highly effective unit drivers training program. Performed direct support maintenance on both light- and heavy-wheeled vehicles. Repaired deficiencies and shortcomings detected during equipment operation and performance of services. Repaired power-assisted brake systems; wheeled-vehicle suspension, steering, and electrical systems; compression ignition engines; and transmission assemblies. Ensured maintenance personnel were qualified and properly trained to work productively, both as part of a team and as individuals utilizing all organizational processes.

Senior Heavy-Wheeled Vehicle Mechanic
November 2000–July 2002, U.S. Army, National Training Center, Fort Irwin, California

Duties/Responsibilities:
Performed maintenance on both light- and heavy-wheeled vehicles, repairing deficiencies. Repaired power-assisted brake systems; wheeled-vehicle suspension, steering, and electrical systems; compression ignition engines; and transmission assemblies.

TECHNICAL TRAINING:

DoD Contract Format and Structure Course, U.S. Army, 2008
Acquisition Reporting Concepts and Policy Course, U.S. Army, 2008
Contracting Officers Representative Overview, U.S. Army, 2008
Contract Terminations Training, U.S. Army, 2008
Acquisition Logistics Fundamentals Course, U.S. Army, 2008
Advanced Leadership Course, U.S. Army, 2005
Automated Air Load Planning System Course, U.S. Army, 2003
Unit Movement Officer Course, U.S. Army, 2003
Airlift Planner's Course, U.S. Army, 2003

ACADEMIC EDUCATION:
Associate's degree, Business Management, Austin Peay University, 2003

SIGNIFICANT CAREER ACCOMPLISHMENTS AND AWARDS:
2005 Distinguished Military Graduate, Advanced Leadership Course, U.S. Army

PROFESSIONAL AFFLIATIONS:
Association of the United States Army (AUSA), member since 2000

SECURITY CLEARANCE: Secret

Curriculum Vitae (CVs)

In some instances, you may find that you need a formal document that highlights more than just your work history or skills and abilities. You may need to list such detail as your publications, presentations, honors, and professional affiliations. In these cases the curriculum vitae, also known simply as CV, works. It is used primarily by those seeking employment in such professions as education, research, medicine, or science. Formats for the CV may vary. The following outline represents one option:

HEADING

[Name, Address, Telephone, and E-mail]

EDUCATION

[Degree(s) earned. List topic of dissertation if applicable. List any other specialized training in your field.]

PROFESSIONAL EXPERIENCE

[Record your work experience relative to the field here.]

PUBLICATIONS

[Subcategorize here using titles such as Books and Book Chapters Written, Book Reviews, Works in Progress.]

PRESENTATIONS

[Indicate whether you were an invited guest speaker. Include the topic of your presentation as well as the date and the name of the organization to which you made the presentation.]

RECOGNITIONS AND HONORS

[List any recognitions and honors you have received.]

PROFESSIONAL ORGANIZATIONS

[List memberships you have in professional societies and associations.]

OTHER PROFESSIONAL ACTIVITIES

[List your memberships on committees of professional societies and any offices you have within those organizations.]

OTHER INDICATORS OF SCHOLARSHIP

[List anything here that doesn't fit neatly in the preceding categories such as contracts received, reviews of your work, and so on.]

Federal Resumes

If you are targeting a position in the federal government, you may find that traditional resume guidelines don't apply. In fact, what you will most likely find is that each position may have different application requirements. You may have the option to use what is known as a federal resume in lieu of a standard application form.

Federal resumes must generally include the following information.

Job Information

Include the announcement number, title, and grade of the position you seek.

Personal Information

Include your full name, mailing address, and day and evening telephone numbers. Also give your citizenship.

Veterans' Preference

Your service in the military may assist you in obtaining preference for employment with the federal government after your life in uniform. This assumes that you were separated under honorable conditions.

If your military service began after October 15, 1976, you must have a Campaign Badge, Expeditionary Medal, or a service-connected disability to claim Veterans' Preference for a federal job. If you are targeting a position in the Senior Executive Service or a job where competition is limited to status candidates (those already in career or career-conditional employment status), Veterans' Preference is not a factor.

To claim a 5-point Veterans' Preference, attach a copy of your DD 214, Certificate of Release or Discharge from Active Duty, or other proof of eligibility to your application packet.

To claim a 10-point Veterans' Preference, attach an SF 15, Application for 10-Point Veterans' Preference, to your application, plus any other requested documentation.

Reinstatement Eligibility

- If you have previous federal employment experience (excluding uniformed military service), you must list the highest federal civilian grade held along with the job series and dates held.

Education

You may be required to submit official or unofficial copies of transcripts for some positions. In most cases, you will nonetheless be required to submit the names and addresses of educational institutions you have attended:

- High school (include the name, city, state, and ZIP code)
- Colleges and universities attended along with your major(s) and types and years of degree(s) earned

Work Experience

You will need to provide a history of your work experience to include the following:

- Job titles
- Duties and accomplishments
- Employers' names and addresses
- Supervisors' names and phone numbers
- Starting and ending dates of employment (month and year)
- Hours worked per week
- Salary earned on an annual, hourly, or monthly basis

You will also need to state on your federal resume whether your present employer may be contacted.

Other Qualifications

Including other qualifications not listed elsewhere on your resume would be to your advantage. For example, list your job-related training courses completed or your job-related skills. Additionally, note any licenses or certificates you have earned as well as any noteworthy honors received.

For more information regarding federal resumes, consult the *Federal Resume Guidebook* by Kathryn Kraemer Troutman for more details. You can also visit her Web site at www.resumeplace. com.

You may also be required to supplement your resume or job application with any number of additional forms, questionnaires, or narratives addressing various knowledges, skills, and abilities, also known simply as KSAs. The level of detail that you supply regarding these KSAs can be related to the level of position you are seeking.

> Please note, and this point is important, criteria differ depending on the agency offering the job.

In many cases, you can use a semifriendly resume builder to help you construct the resume, or you may also create it yourself and then copy and paste it.

Also keep in mind that the application, interviewing, and selection process involved in federal employment, while improving, is still long and tedious. The shift to the National Security Personnel System (NSPS) structure of doing business has not been without glitches, and patience is required.

Step Four: Identify Additional Experience and Include as Appropriate

Just what is considered appropriate experience versus what isn't depends largely on the job. For example, highlighting your superior weapons marksmanship would probably not be a good idea for a senior-level management position within corporate America. If, however, you're applying for a position within law enforcement, it becomes relevant. In such a case, one could even argue that it is more of a job-related skill rather than an optional category.

In any event, be careful about the extras that you may be inclined to include on your resume. Generally speaking, the following types of information are *verboten:*

- Age
- Height
- Weight
- Salary requirements
- Salary history
- Political affiliation
- Religious beliefs
- Marital status
- Condition of physical health

The acid test here is this: Does including this information directly support your objective? If it does, include it. If it doesn't, leave it off and forget what all the so-called experts say. For example, an aspiring model would probably include age, height, and weight. A personnel manager would not.

Step Five: Review, Edit, and Revise Your Resume as Necessary

After you've completed the first draft of your resume, put it away for a day or so. You can easily find yourself a victim of tunnel vision. When that happens, you are usually mortified later to realize you omitted something important from your resume. Just take a break from reviewing and go back to it in a day or so when you can look at it again with fresh, objective eyes.

You are never going to get to a point where your resume is completed. That may be discouraging to hear, but it's the truth. As you apply for different positions, even if they fall in the same career field, you should review, edit, and revise your resume as necessary to best target it for a given opportunity. Taking this step requires a bit more effort, but your resume will stand out from the others if you make the extra effort.

What to Do with Your Resume After You're Hired

The temptation may be great to file away your resume after you've been hired. That's not the best idea. Now that you've spent so much time and effort on it, keep it updated. You never know when you will need it again. Having it available and up-to-date at all times is not only prudent, but is also necessary in the ever-changing world of work.

Resume Writing Tips Worth Reviewing

You need not be a writing guru to develop an effective resume. You simply need to select the most appropriate format and keep in mind the following tips as you craft your document:

- Use power words that clearly identify your skills and experiences.

- Refrain from using personal pronouns such as *I*, *me*, or *my*.

- Use a consistent tense in your sentence fragments throughout your resume.

- Avoid using the random acts of capitalization that are perfectly acceptable in the military. It will be difficult, but follow the English language's rules for proper capitalization.

- Use words that you know and understand; don't try to sound like someone you're not.

- Don't rely solely on your computer's spell- and grammar-checking tools. They may work on one level but not completely.

- Don't create endless sentences by using semicolons. You are not creating a military performance review or copying a job description. Use periods at the ends of your sentence fragments. It's okay to have varying lengths.

- Use appropriate and correct punctuation.

- Keep your resume to no more than two pages, unless directed otherwise by the employer.

- Use an attractive, easy-to-read serif font at 10, 11, or 12 points in size.

- Don't type your resume in all capital letters.

- Don't overformat your resume with bullets, underlines, and bold and/or italic letters, particularly if it is destined for scanning. Scanners don't always pick up the finer formats, and the reader could be left with a resume full of strange symbols rather than your intended formatting.

- If faxing your resume, use plain bond paper rather than heavier stationery.

- If using stationery, keep it conservative in color (white and cream are the best shades to use for easier reproduction purposes).

- If your stationery has a watermark on it (hold it up to the light to see whether it does), insert it in the printer so that the watermark can be read from left to right after your resume has been printed.

- If mailing your resume, use a standard business-sized envelope rather than the oversized variety.

- If you are creating a cover letter to go with your resume, use matching stationery and headings.

- Keep a one-inch margin around your resume. The empty space actually makes your resume appear more attractive and organized than if you attempted to use every inch of space.

- If you are e-mailing your resume to someone, ensure that it gets there not only by attaching it to the file, but also by cutting and pasting it from your word processor onto your e-mail message, just below your e-mail cover letter.

CHAPTER 6

Creating Effective Job Search Letters

At this point in the job search process, you have a clue about what you are supposed to do to land a decent job. You realize that you have to be able to sell your skills, abilities, and experiences as they relate to the position available to a potential employer.

You may assume that the resume is the dedicated workhorse vehicle for accomplishing this feat. No one will dispute the importance of the role of the resume in this process; however, it's not the only written aspect of your job search with the power to influence an employer, positively or not.

Whether the end result is an e-mail or a letter, how you express your words matters in a very big way.

You take your resume seriously. Give your cover letters, thank-you notes, and other job search letters the same respect.

The Cover Letter and Its Parts

You craft the perfect resume for what appears to be the perfect job. Unless it isn't expected of you under the circumstances, you will want to include a cover letter along with that resume.

Your cover letter isn't a novel, and it shouldn't be a mirror image of your resume. It should be brief, no longer than one page, and it should clearly and effectively convince the employer to give your resume the time of day.

If you are e-mailing your resume as an attachment or pasted within the body of a message, the "cover letter" is your e-mail message. Although you can dispense with the heading formalities, you should not dispense with the content protocol.

You may spend a great deal of time creating, editing, and revising your resume. Don't jeopardize your hard-earned chances to this point by breezing through the cover letter without any real thought.

The basic parts of a cover letter are as follows:

- The heading
- The date
- The addressee
- The salutation
- The introduction
- The main body
- The conclusion
- Your signature block

Heading

If you look at the heading on your resume, you'll see your name and your contact information. This is how the heading on your cover letter should also appear. In fact, this heading should match the information and layout of the heading on your resume exactly. Remember, this section should not go into overkill on contact numbers, and it should clearly show the employer how to contact you easily.

If you are sending an e-mail instead, the e-mail header takes care of identifying you at this point. Instead, include the traditional header content in your actual signature block. The same information will also, of course, appear on the top of your attached resume.

Date

After your heading, skip a couple of lines and insert the date in a civilian format. Avoid using abbreviations and military-style formatting in this section as well as throughout your entire cover letter.

The format is a dead giveaway to someone who hasn't transitioned yet, on paper anyhow.

Don't Use:	1 July 2010
	7/1/10
Use:	July 1, 2010

If you are sending an e-mail instead, skip the date. It's in the e-mail header already.

Addressee

Do you know the person you are sending your letter to? If not, you need to go back to square one and do a little investigative work.

Always send your cover letter and resume to an actual person rather than a department title if at all possible. Doing so illustrates your level of genuine interest in the position. Anyone can address a letter to the Human Resources Director.

The candidate who takes the initiative to pick up the telephone or get online to find out to whom the letter should be addressed will stand out from those who didn't. Be certain of correct names, spellings, genders, and addresses while you're looking up information.

If you are e-mailing your cover letter, you can bypass including the addressee in the e-mail itself.

Salutation

Whether you are composing a traditional letter or an e-mail, you will include a salutation line. Make it an effective one.

"Dear Mr. Smith," for example, works just fine.

Typing "Dear Sir or Madam" or "To Whom It May Concern" suggests you are lazy and did not take the time or make the effort to get the right name.

Equally appalling is the practice of assuming familiarity where there is none. "Dear Susan" doesn't impress Mrs. Jones one bit.

If you are not certain about Mrs. Jones's marital status and fear insulting her one way or another, just type "Dear Susan Jones" instead.

Introduction

In the all-important first paragraph, you have the opportunity to get the reader's attention.

Here, you tell the employer specifically why you are writing the letter. Identify the position you are interested in and reveal how you learned about it. Be specific.

Did someone else refer you? If so, consider mentioning that fact here, using your contact's name in shameless vain. Job seekers, be forewarned, however. Invoke the act of name-dropping only if you are confident that the relationship between the two parties is a positive one.

Don't bother opening with "My name is John Smith, and I blah, blah, blah...." Your heading took care of telling the reader your name or, if you're e-mailing, your signature block will.

Main Body

You've set the stage, now you need to shine.

The goal of the main body is to show the employer how your skills match the needs for the position in question. That means you have to know what those desired skills are in the first place. Let's hope you have an idea already. If you are lacking for inspiration on some level, don't worry. You can also use the same words that the employer uses in the job advertisement itself, assuming it is available to you.

The point in the main body is to make a solid connection between you and the job you seek. You want that employer to pick up the telephone or click the Reply button immediately after reading your cover letter and giving your resume the once-over.

The main body of your cover letter should not repeat your resume. You want to build up interest for employers to actually read your resume, and you don't want them to become bored with the same stuff when they do.

Limit the main body to two or three decent paragraphs at the most.

Conclusion

You're almost through! Hang in there. All you have to do is close out this letter, whether you are sending it via e-mail or snail mail.

Your goal in the conclusion is basically to be nice and control destiny at the same time. To get the most power from your punch, include a call to action in which you not only thank the reader for due consideration, but proactively set the stage for future communications.

For example:

> Thank you for your consideration of my qualifications. I will call you the week of September 15 to answer any questions you may have regarding my resume. If you would like to contact me before then, I can be reached at the above telephone number or e-mail address.

Your Signature Block

Surely, after any amount of time in the military, you know all about signature blocks. Your civilian one, however, will not be the quite the same as your uniformed one.

Don't use:	SHARON J. PHILLIPS
	COL, USA
	Director, HQ ANYWHERE, Personnel Directorate
Use:	Sincerely,
	Sharon J. Phillips

Notice the unique lack of random capitalization, use of rank, and mention of current employer in the second example. This is the civilian way. Embrace it.

Sincerely can easily be replaced with other like sentiments such as *Respectfully, Regards, or With Warm Regards.*

In a snail-mailed version, leave five lines between the *Sincerely* (complimentary closing) and your name so that you can sign the letter.

In an e-mailed version, spaces between the two are not necessary.

James Graven

University Avenue #14 ◆ Chicago, Illinois 60609 ◆ (555) 555-5555 ◆ jgraven@myemail.com

February 24, 2010

Alan Spade
Blue Moon Warehouse
5555 Industry Lane
Chicago, Illinois 60608

Dear Mr. Spade,

Please accept the attached resume for your consideration of the Logistics Manager position at Blue Moon Warehouse, which I learned about through your company's Web site (Job# LM201038).

Given the opportunity, I can gladly bring more than 20 years of valuable managerial and technical experience in the field of logistics management right to your doorstep. I offer current expertise in quality assurance, personnel management, property accountability, and warehouse/distribution operations.

Most recently, I worked as supervisory quality assurance monitor in the U.S. Army, where I provided accurate oversight of National Level Stock Records having in excess of 6,000 line items. In this position, I supervised a staff of more than 20 supply technicians and served as the subject matter expert on matters relating to inventory management, warehouse operations, and customer service. In addition to my supervisory and QA background, I am also able to safely and efficiently use forklifts and perform pallet jack operations.

In me, you will find a dependable employee with excellent communication skills and the ability to perform advanced-level supply management functions. Additionally, I am willing to work flexible schedules as needed to successfully manage the workload.

I thank you for your serious consideration of my qualifications, and I look forward to hearing from you soon. I will contact you the week of March 7 to answer any questions you may have regarding my resume.

Sincerely,

James Graven

Figure 6.1: Sample cover letter.

The preceding cover letter shown in Figure 6.1 is clearly and concisely written. It meets all the following cover letter requirements nicely:

- It is addressed to a person, not a job title.
- It uses civilian date formatting.
- It includes a complete heading.
- It offers an appropriate salutation line.
- The introduction clearly sets the stage.
- The main body connects the job seeker with the job.
- A call to action is provided in the conclusion.
- An appropriate ending sentiment is provided.
- A civilian-style signature block is used.

Thank-You Notes

Some unknown wise person once said that it's nice to be important, but it's important to be nice. Sending thank-you notes definitely falls in the nice category, but the benefits you reap don't stop there. Let's examine the concept in more detail, shall we?

Who exactly should you send a thank-you note to, and when should you do it?

You should always send a thank-you note to an employer after an interview. If you interviewed with more than one person, send a note of thanks to each one.

Don't stop being nice there, either. If anyone helps you along the way, send that person a nice note of thanks for his or her assistance.

Contrary to popular belief, sending such notes is not sucking up. This is common courtesy, and it could make the difference in whether you get the job. Not only will you make your mama proud, but you might also reap residual benefits in the process.

You know how it works: When you are nice to someone else who has been nice to you, that person remembers your behavior, and often the resulting goodwill comes back at you tenfold.

Thank-you notes may be sent in a couple of different ways. You can send an informal, handwritten note on a nice piece of stationery. If you do, be sure to write neatly and keep it short.

You can also send an expanded note, a thank-you letter, if you will. The parts of this type of letter resemble that of the basic cover letter:

- The heading
- The date
- The addressee
- The salutation
- The main body
- The conclusion
- Your signature block

The biggest difference between the cover letter and thank-you letter can be found in the main body and conclusion. For specific details on how to create the heading, the date, the addressee, and your signature block, see "The Cover Letter and Its Parts" earlier. Figure 6.2 shows a sample thank-you letter.

Main Body

The main body of the thank-you letter, like the cover letter, should be about one to two paragraphs in length. In it, you can thank the employer for his or her valuable time. Remind the employer of when you interviewed and for which position. You can even give the employer your initial impressions of the job opportunity as it was discussed and remind him or her why you are the right person for the position.

You can also mention anything here that you neglected to mention in the interview or reiterate an important point you don't want the employer to forget.

Melissa Samuel
#55B Fairway Drive
Pensacola, Florida 55555
(555) 555-5555
msamuel@myemail.com

March 15, 2011

Mrs. Donna Walker
General Dynamics
5555 West Overland Avenue
Dulles, VA 55555

Dear Mrs. Walker,

Thank you for your time and insights yesterday during my interview with you for the Programming and Policy Analyst position within the Information Technology Division.

I remain highly interested in this position and hope that you continue to seriously consider me for it. I know that my extensive background of Department of Defense (DoD) and U.S. Air Force foreign language education and training techniques, systems, and programs would be a great benefit to General Dynamics.

As I mentioned, I am also highly experienced in writing and coordinating DoD policies and instructions and would be available for employment on April 15, 2011.

I truly enjoyed meeting with you yesterday and look forward to hearing from you soon. Thank you again for the interview and the consideration.

Sincerely,

Melissa Samuel

Figure 6.2: Sample thank-you letter.

Conclusion

In the conclusion, repeat your gratitude without going overboard. Mention that you are looking forward to a response soon. Finally, if you want the job, just come out and ask for it point blank. Why not? Even if you're not sure you want the job, be confident in this letter that you do. Your goal in an effective job search is to generate choices. You have to have them to make them.

You may send your thoughts in a handwritten note or an e-mail message, but send them. Details count now more than ever, and this is good one to incorporate in your job search.

Networking Letters

Networking, as you already know, is key in your job search. It not only helps you land a job and effectively work it, but also helps you get promoted throughout your career.

A networking letter is simply a flexible tool that helps you accomplish networking on paper or by e-mail. It is a piece of correspondence that you write to someone you know or not, who might be able to help you in your job search.

Networking letters include the same basic cover letter components:

- The heading
- The date
- The addressee
- The salutation
- The main body
- The conclusion
- Your signature block

For specifics on how to complete the heading, the date, the addressee, the salutation, and your signature block, see "The Cover Letter and Its Parts," provided earlier in this chapter.

The main body of the letter itself can be detailed or not. If you don't reference an attached resume (because there isn't one), go into a bit more detail about your qualifications and what you want to do with them.

If you include a resume, don't be as detailed but still give the reader a basic idea regarding your intentions and qualifications.

You may send this letter to someone who has an actual job opening or to someone who can help you get into contact with someone who does. Remember the whole spiderweb effect to networking? It's alive and well here.

Like all job search letters, the networking letter should be kept to a minimum length, with one or two pages being best (see Figure 6.3).

David Jones
22222 Winegarten Drive
Austin, Texas 55555
(555) 555-5555
davidjones@myemail.com

May 1, 2012

Charles Greatman
SAIC, Inc.
2561 Corporate Drive
Vienna, Virginia 12345

Dear Mr. Greatman,

Jaime Winthrop, a mutual acquaintance of ours, suggested that I contact you. She mentioned that you would be a good point of contact for me at SAIC as I consider my future career options after leaving the military.

I am currently in the U.S. Navy and will be available for employment beginning in September 2012. I am seeking employment as a network operations manager and would be interested in discussing potential opportunities at SAIC, Inc. Your company enjoys a distinguished reputation, and I would like to explore the possibility of becoming a member of your team. I have enclosed my resume for your review.

Would you perhaps be available to chat in more detail about possible openings at SAIC in the near future? I would be grateful for the chance to talk with you either over the telephone or in person, at your convenience.

Thank you in advance for your consideration.

Sincerely,

David Jones

Figure 6.3: Sample networking letter.

The Letter Resume

There is a fine line between the networking letter and letter resume (see Figure 6.4). In essence, the letter resume is a detailed cover letter that doesn't include a copy of your resume. You can use it for networking purposes or for applying for a job. The more traditional approach is to simply use the cover letter and resume as the case warrants. On occasion, however, you might find the letter resume a useful tool.

As you can read here, there is slightly more detail in the letter resume. It gets into a few more work-related details as opposed to the networking letter. There is room in your job search bag of tricks and tools for both kinds of letters.

Other Types of Job Search Correspondence

Throughout your job search process and after, there will be occasions for you to compose, or ask others to compose for you, various types of correspondence related to your career. Examples of each are provided for you in this chapter to give you an idea how to word them.

- **You are accepting a job.** You may sign a contract, and that would take care of accepting the offer. If one isn't given to you, put all the details discussed in your letter (see Figure 6.5).

Frances Terry

5555 North Ocean Drive ■ San Diego, CA 55555
555.555.5555 ■ frances.terry@myemail.com

August 8, 2012

Terrence Baumstead
Trace Inc.
5555 South Parkway
Los Angeles, CA 55555

Dear Mr. Baumstead,

David Jansen, a mutual friend, suggested I contact you regarding potential employment opportunities. He mentioned that you were always on the lookout for someone having a solid satellite communications background. I could be that person you seek.

For more than 22 years, I have worked in the defense industry as a member of the U.S. Air Force. Specifically, I manage strategic, tactical, and commercial wideband satellite systems. I have programmatic and operational experience with EHF, UHF, and commercial and military SHF terminals. I also maintain an active top secret security clearance.

In my current position, I work with the Defense Information Systems Agency (DISA), where I manage 10 commercial satellite systems and more than 20 defense satellite communications systems in support of military operations overseas.

Before coming to DISA, I worked closely with the U.S. Air Force-Europe where I effectively supervised more than 30 technicians responsible for the maintenance activities of a major command. In that position, I ensured accurate accountability of a $400,000 budget while overseeing the operation, logistics, equipment modification, and installation of new equipment.

Additionally, I have coordinated and conducted production work and inspected equipment to ensure technical contractual compliance. I also have extensive experience evaluating and rating employee performance.

Throughout my military career, I've successfully worked with others from all over the world to make their voices heard, literally. It's a career path that I wish to continue on as I leave the active military service behind and enter the civilian job market. I would like to discuss the possibility of carrying on that work with Trace if you are receptive to the conversation.

Thank you in advance for your time and consideration.

Sincerely,

Frances Terry

Figure 6.4: Sample letter resume.

Alfred Schmidt
55555 West Tree Place #54
Seattle, WA 55555
(555) 555-5555
aschmidt@myemail.com

April 16, 2011

Mr. Herman James
Media Services Incorporated
2626 Dulles Way
Seattle, WA 55555

Dear Mr. James,

Thank you for the recent opportunity to learn more about the Account Manager position with Media Services Incorporated. I am also grateful for the job offer you extended me for that position at a salary rate of $54,000 per year. I am happy to accept and would like to discuss a start date with you as soon as possible.

Thanks again, and I look forward to working with you.

Sincerely,

Alfred Schmidt

Figure 6.5: Letter accepting a job.

- **You are declining a job.** If you are certain you do not want a job that was offered to you, bow out gracefully (see Figure 6.6). You never know when you may cross paths with an employer again.

Alfred Schmidt
55555 West Tree Place #54
Seattle, WA 55555
(555) 555-5555
aschmidt@myemail.com

April 16, 2011

Mr. Herman James
Media Services Incorporated
2626 Dulles Way
Seattle, WA 55555

Dear Mr. James,

Thank you for extending me a job offer for the position of Account Manager with your company. Although the offer is a generous one, I do not believe it is the right one for me at this time.

Again, thank you, and I wish you the best in finding the right candidate for the position.

Sincerely,

Alfred Schmidt

Figure 6.6: Letter declining a job.

- **You are resigning from a job.** When you are crafting a letter of resignation, don't feel obligated to go into the gory details regarding your reasons for departure. Doing so might well create a bigger situation for you than you intended. Just stick to the basic facts without going into details (see Figure 6.7).

Alfred Schmidt
55555 West Tree Place #54
Seattle, WA 55555
(555) 555-5555
aschmidt@myemail.com

April 16, 2011

Herman James
Media Services Incorporated
2626 Dulles Way
Seattle, WA 55555

Dear Mr. James,

For the past three years, I have enjoyed working with Media Services, Inc., as an Account Manager. During this time, I have had the opportunity to work with a group of true professionals, which makes this letter difficult to write.

My last day with Media Services will be April 30, 2011, as I have accepted employment with another company. I am grateful to you and Media Services for the valuable experiences I've gained these past few years.

Thank you for the opportunities you have provided me.

Sincerely,

Alfred Schmidt

Figure 6.7: Letter resigning from a job.

- **You are asking for recommendation/reference letters.** In the example provided in Figure 6.8, the writer uses "To Whom It May Concern." This salutation is acceptable in this case because this letter is coming from someone else to you for your use in multiple situations. You could also ask your references to provide you dedicated letters to a specific employer, but don't abuse the goodwill of your references while you're at it.

Janet James
4568 South Broadmore Place
Phoenix, Arizona 55555
555.555.5555
janet.james@myemail.com

October 25, 2012

To Whom It May Concern:

I would like to take the opportunity to recommend Sandra David for a management position with your organization. Having been her supervisor for the past five years of her ten-year military career, I feel well qualified to share my insights about her abilities with you.

In her most recent position in the U.S. Air Force, Mrs. David served as the Military Personnel Program Manager for a 500+ strong organization. It was a challenging position, and she handled it extremely well, better than others before her who were even more experienced in the field.

In her tenure as manager, Mrs. David ensured the U.S. Air Force mission in her area of responsibility was adequately staffed with appropriately skilled service members. This was critical to our success. She advised senior leadership about policy changes and implications as necessary. When her research uncovered an outdated practice, she aggressively sought to have it amended through the proper channels.

Mrs. David's organizational and communication skills are exemplary. Her thorough knowledge of the basic concepts, principles, and theories of personnel management, coupled with her ability to work across and outside the organization, has been a genuine asset to our organization. I am certain she would bring the same benefit to yours.

Additionally, while working a full-time position in the U.S. Air Force, Mrs. David has successfully completed an MBA degree and actively volunteered in the military community with the youth sports program as a coach.

I highly recommend Mrs. David for a managerial position in the field of human resources. She will be a wonderful asset to any company lucky enough to hire her.

Please feel free to contact me if you have any questions or wish to discuss this matter in more detail.

Sincerely,

Janet James

Figure 6.8: Recommendation/reference letter.

Cross Your T's; Dot Your I's

Dress your job search letters for success just as you would dress yourself for an interview. They will stand an increased chance of actually being read by others if you take the time to construct them in a professional manner.

Letter Length

All your job search letters should be as brief but as thorough as possible. Try to limit them to no more than one page. In some cases, two might be appropriate, but generally speaking, shorter is better.

Typeface Recommendations and Enhancements

In today's graphic-rich world, you can choose from literally thousands of fonts and type styles. Contain your inner artist and keep your letter simple. Bypass the CHARLEMAGNE STD BOLDS of the font world and stick to these easy-to-read classics in 10, 11, or 12 point:

Times New Roman

Arial

Courier

Contrary to accepted societal dogma, size matters. Adjust your size for easy readability depending on where you are putting the words. For example, if you are e-mailing a letter, you can get away with a smaller font than you could if you were sending a traditional letter on paper.

However your content is delivered, it should be easy to read. It should not be too small or too large. It should be just "write" for the reader.

Enhancements such as bolding, underlines, italics, and graphics are best kept to a minimum. If you simply can't contain your inner artist, subtly mirror the graphics used by the company you are targeting.

For example, suppose the company where you would love to be employed always uses double underlines under the company's name in any correspondence or even on its logo. You might consider incorporating double underlines somewhere on your letter. Or if a particular published job announcement uses bullets or arrows, you could use bullets or arrows similarly.

Associating your content with the company's in this manner could subconsciously suggest to the reader that you already fit in with the organization. Could this be a total stretch in thinking and misuse of modern organizational psychology? Who knows? It wouldn't hurt your chances, however.

Paper Types

Just as there are a number of fonts available to use, there are various paper types as well. As for colors of paper, you have a rainbow of choices. It would be in your best interests, though, to stick with basic white or cream. Basic white photocopies best, and we all hope that is what will happen to your credentials as they are passed around the firm. If you are e-mailing your content, no worries here. If you are faxing your documents, use plain bond paper. Save the 20-20 pound stationery, watermarked specials for other times when you are either mailing or hand-carrying your letters.

R-E-S-P-E-C-T

Give all your job search letters the same respect you give your resume, and you'll be seen as a professional player, serious about landing the right job.

CHAPTER 7

Winning Interview Skills

If you stick with your job search efforts long enough, they will ultimately result in an interview. This is your time to shine and to show a potential employer that you would be an incredible asset to his or her organization. It is also a time for you to fully investigate whether an opportunity is suited to your talents, skills, and taste. A job interview is truly a two-sided event, and if you keep that thought in mind, you'll minimize the stress of it all.

Understanding the Interview Process

You may have sat on military board reviews before, but civilian interviews have nothing in common with them. Keep in mind that there are different *types* of interviews, each having a different purpose. The three basic types are the *informational interview, screening interview*, and *employment interview*. Any one of these types of interviews may occur over the telephone, in person, via e-mail, or using video-teleconferencing technology.

The Informational Interview

The informational interview is an excellent way to gather—you guessed it—information about a particular employer or career field. It is an equally excellent way to network into a circle of influence that could prove far-reaching in your own career endeavors. Don't underestimate the value of such an interview. It could open doors for you like no other.

The Screening Interview

Time is money, and employers don't like to waste either. The screening interview is a useful tool for everyone's mutual benefit. It allows both parties to determine whether any future association is plausible. It can happen in any number of formats, including telephone, e-mail, teleconferencing, or in person. It is often a conversation initiated by someone other than the decision maker, but not always.

The Employment Interview

The employment interview is the mother of all interviews. It is the one that leads (or not) to employment in an actual position within an organization. Employment interviews can be held in a formal or informal setting. They can be conducted by one or more individuals. You can participate in only one interview or in a whole series of them. In short, there is no single definition of what constitutes such an event. That's what makes the whole process so fun, don't you think?

Tips, Techniques, and Tricks of the Trade

Essentially, employers want to know three things about you, even if they don't come right out and say it. They want to know whether

- You can do the job.
- You will do the job.
- You will fit in with their organization.

It's up to you to communicate your ability, willingness, and flexibility.

You can view the interview itself in one of two ways. It can be a stressful occasion for which you fail to prepare. Or you can take the better approach by understanding the interview process for what it truly is.

The interview process is just that—a process. It is an opportunity for you and the employer to meet and find common ground. You both want to make the right choices for your own interests. You can't possibly do that until you learn more about each other. View the interview as a learning experience. You will be questioned, yes. You will also have the chance to ask your own questions.

The key to making the process effective for you is simple research. You must know something about the company and about the position before you interview for it. It is assumed that you have already begun this process because you applied for the job. Now, you need to dig a little deeper so that you look like a serious contender in the face-to-face meeting.

Again, because the point bears repeating, the whole idea of the interview process is to generate choices so that you can make an educated decision concerning your future career after gathering all the pertinent facts. The rest of this chapter breaks down the interview into the proverbial *before*, *during*, and *after* portions and looks at time-honored and proven strategies for success at each stage.

Before the Interview

Successful interviews don't just happen all by themselves. They happen because the job seeker has taken the time to thoughtfully organize and prepare for the event.

Get Your Facts Straight

There is a certain element of excitement involved in actually getting an interview. This small success means that whatever you have been doing in your job search is working. That's a good feeling, and you can easily get caught up in the thrill of it all. In your enthusiasm, don't neglect to get straight the details of the event. For example:

- **When is the interview?** Make sure you have the correct day and time noted.

- **Where will the interview be held?** Do you know where the company is actually located? Is it on the other side of town, and will you need to fight morning rush hour to get there for a 9:00 a.m. interview? Is the interview located in another city? Will you need to carry your interview clothes with you and change somewhere prior to the interview to prevent the "I've been driving for three hours in the middle of summer" look? Be sure that you factor in any additional time needed to get to the interview punctually. Or maybe you need only go as far as your computer's webcam for the big event. Interviews today can happen anyplace, anytime. Be prepared for anything.

- **Who will be conducting the interview?** Try to find out as much as possible about the person who will be interviewing you. If you have been doing adequate research on the company, you should have some idea of where this individual fits into the organizational scheme. Having this bit of information can help you prepare better for the questions that may come your way. For example, if your career is highly technical in nature and your first interview with this company is with a representative from the Human Resources department, you might have to change your wording so that this interviewer knows what you're talking about. You might also be interviewed by more than one person at the same time. This interview situation presents a different scenario for you. Again, having as much information beforehand as possible can help you better prepare.

Dress for Success

In the military, dressing was easy. You wore a specific outfit for specific occasions. You knew which shoes or boots went with what outfit, and everyone was wearing the same color, anyway. Others in the military could take one look at you while you were wearing your uniform and immediately have an idea of how long you had been in the military, which unit you currently belonged to, and what type of training you had accomplished. You were, in a manner of thinking, a walking resume. When you're a civilian, someone may not be able to read you as carefully on first glance, but you will make impressions right off the bat, and they are not easily changed.

By the time you land your first interview, you should be well on your way to establishing your civilian wardrobe. Interview outfits, however, sometimes differ from those you would wear on a day-to-day basis. Bottom line: You want to make a good first impression, and you have only one opportunity to do so. *Dress up*.

Let common sense prevail when you select your interview outfit. For example, if you're applying for a managerial or executive-level job, your attire should obviously fit the occasion. If the thought of matching your socks, shoes, shirt, and skirt or pants terrifies you, you may want to employ the services of a professional shopper at a reputable department store.

Say It Isn't So

In my first civilian job, I conducted interviews with mostly people who were transitioning from the military. I had one individual who asked me what he should wear when he came to the interview with me. I told him to wear whatever he thought would be appropriate to interview for a civilian job. He showed up in his BDUs [Battle Dress Uniform]. He did not get the job. Attire was not the only consideration, but it certainly weighed in the decision.

—*Dale Michaels, Defense Contractor*

Wear a Good Attitude

Don't be fooled. Qualifications are important. Looks help. Attitude, however, can make or break your chances. How you come across to potential employers plays an ultra-vital role in the decision-making process. It can distinguish you from others who want the same job.

Of course, different employers seek different characteristics. Suffice it to say, there is not a one-size-fits-all attitude that will work every time. Specific traits, however, generally serve you well during such situations.

For example, being seen as a team player, contributor, leader, and follower usually doesn't hurt. Perception is reality, and you have the potential to sit in different roles as the needs of your employer require it. This is not to say that you should suck up and be what someone wants you to be just for the sake of acceptance. It is to say that everyone has a boss, and you have to fit into an organization. More often than you might think, that "fit" counts more than having hard-core skills or sought-after degrees.

You probably already know that there is a fine line between confidence and arrogance. Keep in mind that the former is a big plus; the latter is not and is often seen as aggressive. In the military, you might have been a bold, audacious, risk-taking warrior. Hoo-ah. Check it at the door before you leave your house and go to your interview.

In some situations, your military rank can help you find substantial employment after the service, such as in the defense contracting arena. In other arenas, however, your old rank just doesn't count anymore. The playing field is now leveled, and it's up to you to present your best, your true image. Associating your personal identity too closely with your former, or soon-to-be former, rank can be damaging to your civilian career chances.

Consider the Interviewer's Perspective

You may or may not know who will be interviewing you for a position. This person may be a skilled interviewer, able to fairly and objectively decide whether you are the right candidate for the job. On the other hand, this person may not fall into that category. He or she may be unskilled in the interviewing process and may even be intimidated by your skills, abilities, and experiences. You never know what emotional baggage someone else is carrying, and that someone includes the person who might be sitting across the desk from you at your next interview.

If at all possible, determine whom you will be meeting with. Learn what you can about this individual, either through personal contacts or via a company Web site. Taking this step may help you present your qualifications in the best light.

Expand Your Knowledge of the Company

You must already know something about this company because you took the time to submit your resume and/or job application in the first place. Now it is time to examine your level of knowledge about the organization and to add to it as much as possible. You should be able to answer such questions as the following:

- What business is this company really in? Where are its priorities?

- Does the company have good financial fitness?

- Does it have a good reputation within the industry?

- What is the actual size of the company? Where are its offices located?

- Who are the major players in the organization?

- How does the company see itself?

You can gain this type of information a number of different ways. Visit the company's Web site if it has one. Obtain a copy of the company profile from any number of corporate directories or registers (such as Dun & Bradstreet or Standard & Poor's) available at most libraries. Talk to people you may already know who work for the company. Read the papers or magazines where the company's name may appear.

The idea here is to know as much about this organization as possible so that you can ask intelligent questions during the interview. An added bonus is, of course, the fact that you will look as if you took the time to prepare for the interview itself. Taking this action further illustrates the level of your motivation and the qualities you could bring to the organization. Employers like that kind of thing. It makes you stand out from others who want the same job.

Practice Answering Common Interview Questions

If you can count on one thing in an interview, it is that no two will be exactly the same. The human element involved will always keep the matter interesting. Although you may not know every question that will be thrown at you, you can guess that there will be some generally accepted common questions in the mix.

You should have an idea of how to best answer these questions without sounding as though you memorized your answers the night before. To that end, here is a list of potential questions and comments that may start you thinking about their real meanings and what you'd like to say:

- **Tell me about yourself.** Keep it on a professional level here. Don't talk endlessly on the subject of yourself. You might say more than you really need to at this point. This is a great opportunity to tell the employer about yourself. For example:
  - How much experience you have in a given field
  - Any credentials you have relative to the position, specifically ones that make you stand out from the pack
  - Why you are interested in the position
  - Why you are in the career field at all
  - What you feel you could bring to the company
- **How did you learn about this opportunity?** This will tell the employer how well the company's advertising is doing, assuming the position was announced.

- **What do you know about our company?** Your answer to this question will immediately tell the employer whether you are a serious candidate. Obviously, you should be able to answer this with some indication of prior research.

- **What qualifies you for this job?** Again, how well you answer this question will show the employer just how much you know about the position.

- **When will you be able to begin working?** Make sure you have a fix on this date before you're asked the question. If you are on permissive TAD/TDY, you are not supposed to start working on someone else's dime because you are still under Uncle Sam's control. If you are on transition leave (formerly known as terminal leave), it is allowable.

- **Would you consider a different job within this company?** Don't be discouraged by this question. You may have come to the company initially with interest in one job. After interviewing you, the employer may feel that you are not right for the job in question, but he or she may want to apply your skills in another area. Keep your mind open. The other job could be a better opportunity.

- **What specific experience have you had in this area?** Review your resume before the interview. It may have been some time since you last gave your resume a glance. Your interview will be conducted based on what you included in that document.

- **Why did you leave your last employer? (Why are you looking for a new job?)** Craft your answer to this question with a positive tone. You might say that you felt you had accomplished all you possibly could in your last job and you were now ready for new challenges. If you have negative feelings about your last employer (the military), keep them in check. It's never a good idea to badmouth your past employer in front of a potential new one. While intelligent individuals realize there are two sides to every story, such comments could send the wrong signals unnecessarily. You don't want to be marked as a potential troublemaker.

- **What did you like most about your last job? Least?** Keep whatever you choose to say here also in a positive light. For example, you might say that you least liked the number of hours needed to complete your tasks. You could balance that dislike, however, by adding that you recognized the need for putting in those hours due to the job requirements at that time (suggesting that you will do whatever is necessary to get the job done).

- **Tell me about your strengths. Your weaknesses?** Some people find it difficult to talk about their strengths and even more difficult to talk about their weaknesses. If you find answering this question tough, get over it. If you don't sell your capabilities, no one else will. If you are asked about your weaknesses, make sure you describe a "good" weakness as opposed to the "I always come in late for work" variety. An example of a good weakness might be your never-ending diligence to complete a project.

- **Tell me about a time when you failed.** This may sound like a trick question, but it's not. Everyone has had a less-than-stellar work experience at some point. If you are asked this or a similar type of question, make sure you show how you overcame your failure. Doing so will show the employer that you're human and learned from your mistakes.

- **Describe your greatest career achievement to date.** Your answer will reveal to the employer what is important to you professionally.

- **Where do you see yourself in one year? In five?** Everyone should have a plan or at least an idea of one. How you answer this question will show the employer how organized and visionary your thought processes are in this area.

- **Are you flexible?** This one should be easy for anyone in the military. Not to stereotype here, but flexibility is generally one of the strengths associated with a camouflaged lifestyle.

- **Why should I hire you over others who are just as qualified or even more qualified for this job?** If your resume makes you look good (which it probably did to get you to the interview), now is the time to walk the talk. This isn't the time to be overly humble and shy. If you want this job, say so and give good reasons for it.

- **What salary are you seeking?** If the interviewer asks this question in the first interview, defer the question to a later time. Explain that you need to know more about the position and its responsibilities before you can discuss this point.

Know How to Handle Potentially Illegal or Insulting Questions

Interviewers may either be skilled in the art of interviewing or not. Those who are not will sometimes ask questions in a way, unknowingly or not, that may actually be illegal or personally insulting. For example:

- Were you honorably discharged from the military?

- Do you have any disabilities?

- Are you a U.S. citizen?

- How old are you?

- Are you married?

- How many kids do you have?

- What is your religion?

- Who did you vote for in the last election?

- Have you ever been arrested?

- Are you pregnant?

- Were you in Iraq or Afghanistan? What was that like?

- Have you experienced post-traumatic stress disorder?

Whether illegal, insulting, or just too personal in nature, such questions exist. You can try to wrap your head around the ignorance at their roots, or you can get more details before losing your cool.

For example, ask the employer to repeat the question. If the question is stated in the same manner, ask him or her how that information relates to the position. This is a perfectly acceptable response on your part. You might also try to answer the intent (if there appears to be one) of the question rather than the question itself. For example, "Have you been honorably discharged from the military?" might just mean "What branch of service did you serve in?" or "What type of education and training did you receive while you were in the military?" Knowing in advance how you would handle such a situation may pay off in a big way for you later.

Prepare Your Own List of Questions

Remember that the whole point of doing well at an interview is to generate choices for yourself. For this to happen, you have to get information about the company, job, and people who work there in addition to sharing information about yourself. That is the only way you can make a genuinely educated decision about the job later.

To learn as much about the company and opportunity as possible (and to distinguish yourself from the competition), prepare your own set of questions to ask the interviewer. Here are some samples:

- Why is this position now open?

- How would you describe a typical day on the job here?

- Where does this position fit into the organizational food chain?

- What is the working environment like here?

- Where would I be working and what are the expected hours?

- Is there travel involved?

- If I am hired, what would be the three top issues I would be expected to address?

- Are there advancement and training opportunities available within this company?

- What type of salary is typically paid for someone in such a position?

- What characteristics are you seeking in an employee for this position?

- If selected for this position, whom would I be working with?

- What are the goals of this company for the next year? For the next three years?

- When and how are performance reviews conducted?

Show Yourself the Money—and the Benefits

Your first interview for a particular position may not even address the topic of money and benefits. That's not unusual. You should be prepared for it regardless.

Before you meet with a potential employer, know what type of salary and what types of benefits you are seeking. Having said that, try to avoid the topic on a first interview if at all possible. You want to be sure that you are the right person for the job. You don't necessarily know that five minutes into an interview. If you are forced into the discussion, at least be able to deflect the question back on the interviewer or state your requirement in terms of a salary range versus an exact amount.

Chapter 8 provides more insight into this area.

Be True to Yourself

Sometimes, something strange happens to people who are going to be interviewed. They feel an unnatural need to misrepresent themselves.

You don't want to fall for this line of thinking. Yes, making a good impression is certainly important. The last thing you want to do in an interview, however, is present yourself as someone you are not. You must be comfortable in your own skin. That true perception will work far better for you than the "I'm putting on my best face for you, but it's only an act so I can get this job" facade.

A successful interview is just the first step in what is going to be an actual relationship. You will benefit far more from a truthful and realistic beginning than by using the dog-and-pony-show approach. Keep yourself grounded in reality, and you should do just fine.

Review Your Resume

Finally, review your glowing qualifications by pulling out your resume and giving it a once- or twice-over. Make sure you have a ready supply of real-world examples of your strengths to share when the opportunity arises. Remember, employers can read your resume, but they can't read your mind. You have to tell them why you are the right person for the job. They'll appreciate your being specific and giving them actual insight into how you operate on a professional level.

The Day of the Interview

The day of your interview will eventually arrive, and then the fun will begin! The following advice could prove helpful on that long-awaited day—before and during the interview.

Arrive on Time

If you want to make a good initial impression, you really can't go wrong with showing up 10 to 15 minutes before your scheduled appointment. Doing so indicates that you had a clue where to show up in the first place. It also gives you an opportunity to check into the nearest restroom for a final once-over of yourself. If you arrive earlier, you run the risk of being "too early." Arriving late is simply not an option. If something terribly unforeseen should happen to cause such a thing, call the employer as soon as possible with an apology and a good reason.

Recon the Perimeter

Don't kid yourself. Your interview may be scheduled to begin at 9:00 a.m. If you arrive in the office (or wherever) at 8:45 a.m., that is when you can consider your interview as having begun. The person who has the power to hire you may not be directly looking at you, but others who have the ear of that person will.

Use this time to the best of your ability. Be polite, sociable, and charming to *everyone*. You never know who has the real authority in an organization. Job titles can be impressive; however, power doesn't necessarily earn the biggest paycheck.

Pay Attention to Your Body Language

In front of a military board, you would wear an impeccable uniform and have your eyes front and center, your back erect, and your hands stiffly at your side. Relax! Civilian interviews may be stressful, but you won't be required to exhibit the same body language. In fact, doing so could even subliminally hurt your chances for serious consideration.

Good body language tips include the following:

- **Be dressed for the occasion.** You want to feel comfortable in your own skin, and an extension of that skin is found in your clothes. If you look good, you feel good. This is half of the "first impression" battle alone. If you feel as though you need further guidance in this area, read the section titled "Dress for Success" earlier in this chapter.

- **Offer a firm and confident (not bone-crunching or sweaty) handshake.** If you find that you are nervous, casually wipe your palm on your pants leg or skirt before you shake your interviewer's hand.

- **Maintain good posture.** Good posture means sitting straight and leaning a bit forward toward the interviewer to emphasize nonverbal interest in what he or she has to say to you.

- **Maintain good eye contact.** This doesn't mean staring down your future employer. It does mean appearing interested. The eyes, it has often been said, are the windows to your soul. Be sure your soul presents itself in a professional and interested manner. It's okay to blink occasionally.

- **Refrain from nervous habits.** Maybe you are a finger or toe tapper. Maybe you continuously twirl a strand of your hair. Maybe you stutter under pressure, nervously (and endlessly) tap your pen against a table, or swivel in a chair that will allow you to do so. Whatever your vice, try to be aware of how annoying it can be during an interview. These habits take the attention off you and your wonderful qualifications and put it on your distracting defense mechanisms.

Listen

Listening is a true skill in and of itself. It requires actual concentration on your part, and that isn't always easy to muster when you find yourself in the interview seat. After the interview, you will need to fully evaluate the viability of this opportunity. You won't be able to effectively do that if your nerves, excitement, or lack of concentration get in your way. If taking notes helps you, do it. It's generally acceptable to do this during the interview. Always ask the permission of the person who is conducting the interview first and keep your notes brief but understandable to you later.

Embrace the Silence

Silence, intentional or not, is a potential interview reality and could happen for a couple of reasons. Maybe the person conducting the interview is evil in nature and wants to watch you squirm. Or maybe a phone rings, a coworker pops in to say hello, or the interviewer just loses his or her train of thought. The *why* isn't important. How you handle it is, however. You have options:

- **Option A:** Do nothing. Be brave. Sit firm and the interviewer will catch a clue that you will not be intimidated. Result? Score one for the job seeker.

- **Option B:** Babble the moment away with inane chatter simply because you feel the silence must not exist. Result? Minus one for the job seeker.

- **Option C:** Wait a respectable amount of time and then intelligently bring the conversation back around. You might do this by asking for clarification of a previous point or reminding the interviewer of a particular skill or experience you have that can work for the company. Result? Bonus points for the job seeker.

If You Want the Job, Ask for It

If, after what you've learned during the course of the interview, you decide that you would potentially like to have this job, ask for it. You have nothing to lose and only a choice in the matter to gain. Live on the edge.

Control the Future

Before you leave the interview, it is perfectly acceptable to ask when a selection will be made and when the company would like to see someone sitting in that position. If the interviewer can provide this information to you at this point, you will have a clearer picture of the hiring timeline.

After the Interview

One of the biggest mistakes job seekers make is to fail to follow up. When the interview is over, you must continue your strategic efforts to obtain the job. You should certainly send a thank-you letter or note. (Chapter 6 has more information on this topic.) You could also make a follow-up call in a week or so to see how the selection process is progressing. You don't want to stalk the employer, but you want to keep your name fresh in his or her mind.

Send a Thank-You Note

Never underestimate common courtesy. Writing or typing a thank-you note is a simple thing, and yet so many job seekers neglect to do it. This act not only shows that you have good manners, but also gives you the opportunity to reinforce your enthusiasm and to remind the employer that your ever-so-available and relevant qualifications match his or her needs perfectly. Writing this note also affords you the opportunity to mention anything you might have neglected to mention during the interview.

Don't ignore the potential power of this job search tool. You'll make your dear old mum proud, and you just might gain the edge over your competition. To get the best use of this tool, send it to the person or persons who interviewed you on the day of or the day after the interview.

Chapter 6 provides a sample thank-you letter if you require further guidance in this area.

Follow Up

A week or so after sending your thank-you letter, call the person who interviewed you. Make sure he or she received your note of thanks and reiterate your interest in the position. If you don't already have an answer to the time frame-for-selection question from the interview, inquire about it now.

The whole idea behind the concept of follow-up strategy is to keep your name fresh in the mind of the employer. You are a potential candidate. You are the best candidate. You need to make sure the employer knows that you feel this way.

There's nothing wrong about being persistent. If you want the job, you need to make your best effort to get it. That means you don't sit around waiting for fate to reward you. You get out there and try your best to influence fate so that you will have the job you want or the choices you desire.

Continue Your Job Search Efforts

You might want the job you interviewed for more than anything else in the world. Great. If you've done everything right and if the moon and stars are all aligned, you might very well just be waiting for the perfect offer itself. But...if your luck is off by one iota, you need to continue your job search efforts. Dare I remind you of the cliché, "Don't put all your eggs into one basket"? If you've ever gone house hunting, this concept will be crystal clear to you.

Who's the Family Member Now?

Nothing is more frustrating than feeling as if you have to settle for what's available in the job market. As a family member who may have moved frequently with your active-duty soldier, sailor, or marine, you are probably more than familiar with the concept of "settling." Now is the time to stop settling. There will be no more transfers to some post located in the middle of nowhere, where jobs seem nonexistent. You will no longer have to craft an answer to the inquiring, if not illegal, "How long are you planning to live here?" question often asked by potential employers who suspect that the military will whisk you away after you are adequately trained on the job. As a family member, you now find yourself at the threshold of a new place in your own career path. Maybe it's time for your spouse to follow you around. Maybe it's time for you to rethink your own professional goals and plot a new chart for reaching them. This is not just another transfer time. This is a new beginning. Full speed ahead!

Bonus Tips for the Onscreen Interview

If a job interview finds you smiling into your webcam rather than sitting across the table from an interviewer, consider the following tips to see you through the experience successfully:

- Before connecting online, clear the room of anyone else. You want to project a professional image, and your child's toys have no place in the picture. Nor does your child, your spouse, or your best friend. Make everything the interviewer will see appropriate to the moment.

- Understand how to connect to the interview before you do so. You don't want to look technologically incompetent when you're trying to impress. Likewise, have your sound situation in check. Know that your microphone works clearly.

- Use your eyes. You will "listen" with them in this setup.

- If you are able to keep an eye on yourself during the interview in picture-in-a-picture function on the screen, do so.

- Above all, treat this interview just like one that would happen in person. Know your stuff. Present the best image possible and be yourself.

CHAPTER 8

Negotiating Job Offers

No doubt about it. Being offered a job is a real thrill. It is a signal of success. It means that you did your part well in the job search and an employer wants to bring you on board with the company. Maybe there is even more than one employer out there vying for your presence. (May you be plagued with such problems throughout your whole career!)

The temptation to accept any offered job right away is great. With so many layoffs being a part of the corporate landscape these days, it seems as though grabbing the first offer makes sense, doesn't it?

Doing so means you can just get on with things and let life take its natural course. After all, bills have to be paid, children must be fed and clothed, and the sooner you can land a decent job outside the military the better, right?

Maybe. Maybe not. One thing is certain. There is more at stake here for you to consider than the depressing headline du jour. You need answers to some questions before you accept or decline a job offer.

For example, is it the right job for you? Should you say thanks, but no thanks and just wait for a better offer to materialize? Would that be wise? Or should you snatch this one and keep looking on the side for your ideal job? How do you know you're getting a good offer to begin with, anyway?

No one is discounting the harsh economic realities of today, but your reality of everyday must also be one with which you can comfortably live.

As you begin your analysis of a particular offer or of multiple offers, take comfort in the fact that if you do accept a job and ultimately discover that you don't like it (or vice versa), the world will unbelievably not come to a screeching halt. You will simply have to find another job. This will not be issue for you because, by the time you finish this book, you will know how to find a new job effectively.

Evaluating the Offer

First things first. Do you have the offer in writing? If you don't, you may not have a valid offer. Ask for it on paper. Most companies extend their offers to potential candidates in writing anyhow. Doing so protects them and protects you.

If you're dealing with a company that has made a verbal offer to you and it is waiting for your acceptance or declination, put the terms discussed in writing yourself and secure appropriate signatures on the document. Extreme? Perhaps, but it's better that way. Don't worry about offending anyone. This is business, and employers will understand. If they do not understand and become offended, maybe you should reconsider whether you would want to work for such a company in the first place.

After you have been offered a position, you can assume that a company *wants* to hire you. The proverbial ball is now in your court, and it's up to you to decide whether you want to play the game.

Looking at the offer from two different angles may be helpful. First, do you really want the job? Second, can you and the employer come to an acceptable compensation package?

Do You Really Want the Job?

Clearly, there is a distinct possibility that you want this job; otherwise, you wouldn't be subjecting yourself to this whole gut-wrenching process. In the heat of the moment, however, don't make the mistake of accepting just any job. Accept the one that is right for you and your family.

Now is the time to carefully examine all the information you have gathered, from all sources, about the company and about the job itself. Identify those "deal-breakers" up front so that if you are confronted with them, the decision to say no will be a no-brainer. Make sure you have a decent grasp on the job responsibilities and duties and make sure they are as good of a fit for you as possible.

The following Job Offer Initial Evaluation Checklist will enable you to effectively evaluate up to three job offers at once.

Job Offer Initial Evaluation Checklist

Factor	A	B	C
(Check the block to indicate a "yes." Leave blank for "no.")			
Have an actual job offer in writing for a position	❑	❑	❑
Have informed employer when decision will be made	❑	❑	❑
Possess a clear understanding of the actual work responsibilities	❑	❑	❑
Skills and abilities are a match for those responsibilities	❑	❑	❑
Know where this job fits on an organizational level	❑	❑	❑
Know who would be immediate supervisor/subordinates	❑	❑	❑
Opportunity supports overall career goals	❑	❑	❑
Employer has a good industry reputation	❑	❑	❑
Employee turnover rate is low at this company	❑	❑	❑
Job security appears to exist	❑	❑	❑
Satisfied with the actual job location	❑	❑	❑
Accepting the job would fit my family's needs	❑	❑	❑
Relocation a possibility at some point	❑	❑	❑
Travel a possibility	❑	❑	❑
Comfortable with the stated work schedule	❑	❑	❑
Training and development opportunities exist	❑	❑	❑
Internal/external advancement possibilities exist	❑	❑	❑
Competitive base salary being offered	❑	❑	❑
Adequate benefits package offered	❑	❑	❑
Know how often salary reviews conducted	❑	❑	❑
Understand company policy on cost-of-living factor	❑	❑	❑
Know how often performance reviews conducted	❑	❑	❑

After each interview, take the time to review the preceding list and address the points identified. Go a step further and look at the list *before* you go to the interview to be sure all those points are covered.

If you receive multiple offers, you may consider yourself fortunate or tortured. In either event, multiple offers are a reality, and a situation that is better to find yourself in than the opposite. The following matrix may assist you if you find yourself comparing multiple offers.

Comparison Matrix					
Complete one sheet for each job and then compare the numbers. Use this rating scale: 0 = Doesn't Apply 1 = Unacceptable 2 = Acceptable 3 = Highly Acceptable 4 = Outstanding					
Factor	**0**	**1**	**2**	**3**	**4**
Competitive salary					
Comprehensive benefits package					
Signing bonus and/or other perks					
Position level within company					
Skills a good match for qualifications					
Advancement opportunities					
Company reputation					
Work environment					
Corporate culture similar to own					
Job location/commute time					
Work schedule a personal/family fit					
Travel requirements acceptable					
Job appears to have security					
Subtotal					
TOTAL SCORE FOR THIS OFFER					

Photocopy the preceding sheet for each job you are considering. Using the legend provided at the top of the form, assign a score for each of the listed items. After you've plugged in all the numbers for each item on the list, add the totals. Do this for each position you are considering and then compare the numbers between the jobs. The numbers won't lie. The job prospect having the highest score will represent the one that has most of the characteristics you have deemed important. Only you can decide, however, if it is the job you will actually select.

Can You and the Employer Agree on an Acceptable Compensation Package?

Certainly, salary is a big deal. In our ever so superficial society, it is how we keep score professionally. You may or may not subscribe to that line of thinking, but the facts are still there. To many, the higher the salary offered, the more enticing the job sounds.

You need to remember, though, that the total compensation package is not made up of salary alone. It includes salary plus benefits. You need to evaluate the whole package and not just the base dollar figure.

Show Me the Money: Salary Expectations vs. Salary Realities

Anyone who has ever thought about transitioning from the military has heard the story about the specialist who left the military after his first tour was up only to be hired by a tech firm offering him a $100K+ job. Then there's the one about the senior officer who became a high-speed management consultant for a defense contractor making goodness knows how much money.

Certainly, good fortune, timing, and connections have helped many job seekers land wonderful positions. I hope those attributes will assist you as well, but don't count on them alone. You have to do the legwork here, so start asking yourself the relevant questions.

For example, what career field are you targeting, and how much marketable experience do you have in it? Where are you physically targeting a job? Cost-of-living surveys say that salaries are higher in metropolitan areas than in the middle of nowhere. If you don't believe that, go online and see for yourself. Check out www.salary.com, www.payscale.com, or www.homefair.com and do a little comparison-shopping. You'll be amazed. Certain parts of the country demand higher wages than other parts simply because of cost-of-living differences. Some companies, however, have established their pay structures based on national rather than regional averages. They do this because this structure facilitates the transfer of employees internally without the continual need for salary adjustments. How do you find out? Ask the employer. After you have been offered a job, the door is wide open for discussing all the finer details, from salary to benefits. Nothing is off-limits at this point.

The bottom line is that you want to be paid competitively for what your skills and experiences are worth in the marketplace. Note here that I didn't say "what you are worth." As tempting as it may be, do not equate your personal worth with any salary figure being offered to you. They are two distinct issues, and clouding them will only promote an unhealthy mental attitude for the long run.

Salary negotiation should be an area where everyone wins. You and the employer should both walk away from a successful negotiation process feeling professionally pleased. Knowing when to feel this way, however, can be dubious at best. What you need to do, before you ever find yourself at an interview, is research the topic as much as possible. Know what someone in your career field, working in the location(s) you are targeting, and sharing your level of expertise makes.

You may have to be creative to find out this type of information because the subject of salaries earned is not as open a topic as in the military. In fact, in some companies discussing the topic with other employees could be grounds for dismissal. On the other hand, some employers readily publish their pay scales. To locate such information, try the following:

- Research any number of national, state, and/or industry-specific salary surveys available on the Internet or through your local library. Business publications, trade associations, and professional organizations usually publish annual salary surveys. For example:

  - Dun & Bradstreet's Million Dollar Database (www. dnbmdd.com)

  - Standard and Poor's Register of Corporations at www2. standardandpoors.com

  - Mergent's Industrial Review, formerly Moody's Industrial Manual (www.mergent.com)

- Thomas Register of American Manufacturers (www. thomasnet.com)

- Ward's Business Directory available in your library's reference room

- Consult the U.S. Department of Labor's *Occupational Outlook Handbook* online at http://stats.bls.gov/OCO and the *Career Guide to Industries* at www.bls.gov/oco/cg.

- Utilize cost-of-living and salary calculators available online at reputable Web sites. Three good ones, among many out there, are as follows:

  - www.salary.com

  - www.homefair.com

  - www.payscale.com

- Study want ads of online job banks and in newspapers, which often list salary ranges. One good online source is www. newspapers.com.

- Talk discreetly to others you know have an idea of such information.

- Access the National Compensation Survey online at www.bls. gov/ncs and the Occupational Employment Statistics at www. bls.gov/oes.

Salary Negotiation Basics and Tips

If you have effectively researched salary norms that may apply to you, you are at the point where you can plan a realistic negotiation campaign. Such a campaign involves having a genuine understanding about negotiation basics. Keep in mind that you and the employer should agree on the following:

- What the responsibilities are for the job you are being offered

- What the going rate is for such a position in the current market

- What you are being offered, salary-wise, for this position by the company

- How future salary increases are calculated

169

The process will end in one of four ways:

- You get the salary you want when you ask for it.
- You get part of the salary you want.
- You accept the offered salary as is.
- The company withdraws the offer.

It would be to your advantage to know before the process begins how comfortable you see yourself with each ending. Only you can set the risk level for yourself.

Here are some additional tips regarding the salary negotiation process:

- Be able to express your salary requirements in any terms such as annual, monthly, weekly, daily, and even per minute.

- Let the employer bring up the subject of compensation first. It usually isn't a topic of discussion until after you've been offered a job.

- Remember, you are in the best position to negotiate *before* you actually accept a job.

- If you are asked what your salary requirements are early in the interview, defer your answer until you have learned more about the responsibilities of the position. Some employers use this tactic to screen out candidates having unacceptable salary ranges.

- Some employers request a salary history for additional use as a screening tool. They want to know what you've worked for in the past so that they can base future offers on that amount. Avoid providing this kind of information if at all possible.

Theoretically, you want to be offered more than you've been making. Indeed, the military isn't famous for its high-paying jobs despite the propaganda designed to convince you otherwise.

Skills and expertise that you've acquired while in uniform, however, can be a totally different story. If you are asked for such information, explain to the employer that, no offense intended, you would rather discuss the current position in light of its qualifications and your match for them.

Realize, of course, that not providing such information could result in a withdrawal of an offer. If you agree to provide an employer with a salary history, an example of one is provided for you here. Be sure you provide the "salary" from the military that includes the cost of your benefits as well. If you don't know what that is, contact your finance office for more information.

Samuel Taylor

5248 Manassas Drive, Norfolk, VA 55555   (555) 571-5555

Salary History

Job Title	Employer	Annual Salary
Satellite Network Engineer	U.S. Army	$65,000
Operations Manager	U.S. Army	$57,000
Personnel Supervisor	U.S. Army	$50,000
Communications Technician	U.S. Army	$45,000

- If you are asked what your salary requirements are after learning more about the job, answer the question with a question. For example:

  Employer: Tell me, what type of salary are you seeking?

  Job seeker: What range of salary are you willing to pay for this position?

  Don't play verbal ping-pong on the issue. If you must be the first to come up with a range, add at least 10 to 15 percent onto the highest end of your acceptable salary range.

- Be realistic. Understand that employers usually have a salary range that they can honestly offer. You will either like that range or not. Make a counteroffer if you are not satisfied with the one put before you. If you still can't get to that happy meeting point, be willing to say thanks but no thanks and walk away.

- Couple your counteroffer with reasons why your skills are worth the extra money.

- Realize that after an offer is made to you, the negotiation process is only beginning. Asking for more after an offer has been made is perfectly acceptable. You will either get what you ask for or not.

- Remember that benefits and perks are also negotiable.

- Provide suggestions to the employer if necessary.

- Realize that the salary you accept will more than likely represent the basis for your future salaries.

- Be prepared to back up any requests for a high salary with solid supporting facts. You should be paid more because _____ (you fill in the blank).

- Maintain a positive and professional attitude throughout the process. How you negotiate your own salary and benefits may suggest to the employer how you will perform on the job. There is no reason to be confrontational. Cooperation is key.

- Embrace silence in the negotiation process. You don't have to immediately respond to an offered range. Give the offer due consideration on the spot and don't be tempted to fill in awkward silences with words. The employer may increase the offer in the process or give you more information why it is what it is to begin with.

- Ask the employer about the company's salary review policy. Perhaps you can also negotiate a raise at a future date. Inquire about salary increases as well.

- Inquire about the availability of a severance package.

- Don't accept or reject an offer immediately after it has been made. Ask for a day or two to think it over.

- If you are considering multiple job offers, use the offer of one judiciously against the offer of another in the attempt to arrive at a better place on the more desirable offer.

Benefits and Perks: The Other Half of the Salary Picture

Benefits and perks are just as important in a compensation package as the base salary and may be negotiated as such. It would be to your advantage to first settle on the salary portion and then examine the benefits and perks as additional items.

Following is a brief list of potential benefits to consider aside from the basic offered salary.

Compensation-Related Benefits

Ask your employer about any payments you may receive in addition to your salary:

- **Commissions:** In addition to your base salary, are commissions available? What is the percentage? Earning commissions is usually a possibility if you work in sales or business development.

- **Sign-on bonus:** Keep in mind that signing bonuses are taxed as regular income.

- **Performance bonus:** Does the company offer a performance bonus? Are there other types of compensation, such as a year-end bonus?

- **Relocation allowances:** If accepting a position involves any type of commute, you may be offered an additional incentive for such travel time. If a major move is involved with your acceptance of a job, be sure to inquire about any additional assistance potentially available to you. Depending on your level of employment, you might find that a company is willing to pay for any expenses you incur as a result of selling or purchasing a new home. Some companies even cover the cost of your new driver's license, necessary utility hookups, or even employment assistance for your spouse.

- **Financial planning and tax assistance:** Some companies, particularly if you are working abroad for them, provide financial planning and tax assistance.

- **Expense account:** Does the company offer an account to cover the cost of your work-related expenses? This might be an issue of high importance if you work out of your home for the company. In such a case, your personal rent or mortgage might be considered a business expense as well as your telephone, Internet service, and automobile.

Paid Time Off

Go ahead and mourn the loss of the annual 30 days of leave you received in the military. You probably won't be seeing that ever,

ever again. However, you should expect to receive some time off in your new job:

- **Vacation/sick/personal days:** How much leave can be earned and on what schedule? For example, you may be eligible for only one week of vacation and only after having worked for the company for a specific length of time. Generally, the longer you work for a firm, the more vacation days you may be allowed. Some companies offer vacation, sick, and personal days. Others may just offer a set number of days, and you must fit your vacation, doctor appointments, and other errands into them however you want.

- **Funeral/bereavement:** Most firms offer you up to three days of paid leave to attend the funeral of an immediate family member.

- **Legal obligations:** If you must serve time in the reserves, find out whether the employer supports this in practice because it should by law. Employers are also obligated to allow you paid time to perform jury duty.

Health, Dental, and Vision Insurance

In the military, when you or someone in your immediate family needed to see a doctor, you called the dispensary or the military hospital and usually made a same-day appointment. Unless you incurred an overnight stay, you generally walked away from that visit without much, if any, damage to your own wallet. That is not necessarily what will happen to you as a civilian.

As you consider the health, dental, and vision insurance benefits offered to you, make sure you understand the answer to these questions:

- How much will each of these benefits actually cost you?

- When does coverage begin?

- Will you have flexibility to change any selected policies at a later time?

- Do you have flexibility in designing your own plans?

- What happens to your coverage should you leave the company?

- Do you or your family have any pre-existing medical conditions you need to consider?

Financial Benefits

Following are questions to ask about specific financial benefits:

- **Life insurance:** Is life insurance a company-paid benefit? What is the cost of additional coverage for yourself or family members, if available?

- **401(k):** Are matching 401(k) funds offered by the company? If so, at what percentage? What are the contribution limits? When are you considered fully vested in the program?

- **Stock options:** Is there a discount available for purchase of company stock? Are you allowed to buy and sell? Is there a commission fee?

- **Education and training:** Is tuition assistance available for you or family members? How is the program managed? Are initial out-of-pocket expenses a possibility? Are memberships in professionally related organizations/associations paid for by the company?

- **Personal care:** Examples of personal care benefits may include subsidized or onsite child care, elder care, fitness facilities, or other similar items.

Work-Related Benefits

Employers may offer additional benefits, such as the following:

- **Flexible work schedules and telecommuting:** Depending on the nature of your employment, you may have the opportunity to adjust your work hours or to work out of your home. If these possibilities interest you, be sure to inquire about them during your interview.

- **Severance package:** The last thing you are probably thinking about as you consider a new job is what would happen if you lost your job. Considering the subject of a severance package hardly seems like a positive thing to do, but in the event it actually happens, you will be endlessly happy that you did think about it. Not all companies offer this, and there is no standard package. It doesn't hurt to ask.

- **Perks:** Are you eligible for any additional perks such as a company-paid cell phone, automobile, or credit card?

Making the Decision: Using Your Gut

Knowing how to effectively establish a realistic salary range and negotiate the base salary plus benefits will do you no good unless you can come to a decision. The last phase of any negotiation process is the ultimate moment when you need to actually accept or decline a job.

Timing is critical, and either you have to be willing to accept a job with the caveats discussed in this chapter, or you need to be able to walk away and not look back. In other words, it's show time and you have to play.

In the end, if you are offered a position, only you can decide whether to accept it. You should listen to your gut instincts because they will rarely steer you in the wrong direction. Unfortunately, you don't have the benefit of looking into a crystal ball to see whether you are making the right decision for the long run. You'll just have to look at the facts, trust your instincts, and take your chances. The worst thing that will happen is that you make the wrong decision and end up looking for another job. The world will not stop spinning; life will go on.

You now know how to conduct an effective job search, and you will use these skills throughout your post-military professional life.

CHAPTER 9

On-the-Job Survival Skills

You did it. Despite the economic gloom and doom broadcast 24/7 to the world in general, you have a job, are happy about it, and are soon to receive your first paycheck. Don't spend it all in one place. In fact, you might want to keep in mind a few cold, hard facts as you begin to enjoy your new career as a true blue civilian.

The Basic Facts

Fact #1: Your new job is not perfect.

At first, it may seem that way, but the "honeymoon" will eventually end. You'll see your new job for what it is, and although you may genuinely like it, it is just another step along the way in your career. It will have good days and bad ones, not unlike your life in uniform.

Fact #2: This won't be your last job.

Although it may be a good job, it probably won't be your last one. Chances are good that you will change employers several times over the course of your career. Accept this fact and keep your resume updated at all times. You never know when you will need it for an internal opportunity or something bigger and better elsewhere.

Fact #3: Somewhere along the way, you may work for or be a peer of someone you considered your lowly subordinate in the military or would have if that person had been in uniform.

Yes, it sucks to be you. The sooner you accept the fact that the position you held in the military doesn't play into the civilian equation, the better you will be for it. There may be times when you will be given due credit and respect for your past military career. Just don't count on it getting you by completely in the civilian scheme of things. Own up to the fact that you're in a whole new world and get on with your work.

Fact #4: You will have a learning curve.

Life is going to be different. The concept of military rank and all that it entails is out the window now. Instead, you will have to depend on your charming personality, savvy skills, and business acumen to see you through the day successfully.

Expect, for example, to learn a whole new business vocabulary and do your best to leave your military one behind. Put a quarter in a jar every time you say "hooah," "semper fi," "carry on," or "above all."

Essential Strategies for Success

Your civilian success will depend on your ability to get the job done efficiently and effectively. The rest of this chapter provides you with a handful of powerful and proven strategies to use as you continue your upward career progression.

Strategy #1: Keep Your Mouth Closed and Your Eyes Open

You may have known everything in your last job, but this is not that job. Despite what may be your level of expertise in a particular career field, you are still the new person in the company and have a thing or two to learn. Don't be too hard on yourself in the beginning. Make an effort to observe how people in your company interact with one another. Let others around you get to know you a bit as well. Your environment has changed for sure, but so has theirs. This is the start of a new relationship for all involved. It will no doubt be a good one, but don't expect it to be bump-free.

Remember the Good

When you start your new job, remember the good attributes that the military taught you about being at the appointed place at the appointed time, manners, respect, sense of urgency, and so on. Forget, however, the hoo-ah military jargon and don't be overaggressive.

—Dale Michaels, Defense Contractor

Strategy #2: Check Your Inner Napoleon at the Door

You will, of course, have your mark to make. Depending on the nature of your new position, you might want to consider holding on to that thought for a few months.

Walking in on day one and changing everything to mirror your grand vision may not be as welcome in the civilian world as it was accepted in the military. If you insist on changing everything your first month on the job, you may find yourself disliked quickly within the organization by your peers or even your supervisors. In essence, you are nonverbally communicating to them that they haven't had a clue and have been doing business wrong all along.

Your grand vision may indeed be the correct one for the company, but wait a respectable time before making your changes. Earn your credibility with others first; that way, you make the business of making changes easier for everyone.

Changes

Don't try to make changes too fast. The civilian world is not used to it.

—Laurie Davis, Women's Health Consultant

Strategy #3: Don't Gossip

Gossip happens in every civilian office just as it did in the military. If you have the skill necessary to filter out the fluff from the fact, gossip can be an invaluable, unofficial management tool. Listen to it. Analyze it. Laugh along with it inside silently, but avoid adding your two cents at this time. If you are new to the organization and don't have established relationships with everyone already, gossiping can backfire on you in a heartbeat. Make it a point to stay above the fray at this time.

Professional alliances made too early may disadvantage you later. You've watched *Survivor*. You know the deal.

At this stage, you don't know all the history between coworkers, and you haven't got a clue where the proverbial bodies are buried. Get to know everyone on equal footing first and give others the same opportunity with you, lest you end up being one of those bodies.

Strategy #4: Be a Joiner

You don't have to become the leader of the social pack in your new position, but you should try to participate on some level. If you drink coffee and there is a coffee fund, ante up your share. If all your coworkers meet for lunch once a week, make an effort to join them. Chip in for baby gifts and promotions. These are examples of seemingly insignificant events that, in the long run, make a group of people a team. You know this from wearing a uniform.

Take It Easy

The civilians that I have worked with are very laid back compared to being in the military. No one is in a rush or trying to stay busy. It's a different mindset.

—Steve Martin, Technical Instructor, General Dynamics

Strategy #5: Get Over Yourself

In the military, an admin clerk might have been responsible for making your travel plans. In this world, that fun task may fall to you. Likewise, you may be your own secretary, supply clerk, and/or event organizer. The grunt work may have your name all over it. Get over yourself and drive on.

Strategy #6: Build and Solidify Your Power Base

Learn everything you possibly can and be of assistance to anyone who needs help. By making yourself indispensable, you build a power base that may span varying levels of responsibility, and that is a good base to build. Power, within an organization, doesn't necessarily rest with the person holding the most impressive job title or making the most bucks. It rests with the person who is well connected, knowledgeable, available, and willing to contribute. You want to be that person or be best friends with that person.

Strategy #7: Be on the Lookout for Your Next Job

Suggesting that you look for your next job after you've begun your new one may sound counterproductive. It's not.

In the military, you had a relatively set career path. Maybe you enlisted or were commissioned and chose that path from day one to retirement. Maybe you joined the military and figured out that it wasn't where you wanted to be forever. Either way, the career structure of that path was there. You punched the right tickets, and you theoretically progressed.

Your work is not always as cut-and-dried in the civilian workplace. You are the one who has to chart your career path. You may be lucky enough to have individuals on your side to assist you in this area, but the majority of the responsibility for its success depends on you. Don't expect the human resources department or your supervisors to hold your hand here. You are the one who cares the most about your upward progression. Everyone else is probably looking out for himself or herself.

The bottom line is that you need to always keep your eyes open for the next step. That step may exist within the new company you have selected, or it may not. You may not even consider leaving your current job for years to come, or you may bail at the first opportunity. You would be doing yourself a career favor, however, to be aware of what's out there periodically. Business can change on a dime. If you don't have the proverbial Plan B, you might find yourself at a significant disadvantage.

Strategy #8: Keep Your Skills Current

Planning for future opportunities will do you no good unless you have the skills necessary to compete for those jobs. Likewise, success in your current position will demand that you keep up-to-date on the required competencies. Investigate training opportunities in your new organization. Take advantage of every bit of learning available to you. Explore self-directed opportunities as well. Maybe it's time to examine your academic history and improve upon it. Take this one piece of your professional self and put it under a microscope. What condition is it in now, and how can it be improved? Maintaining and enhancing your skills will benefit the goals of the organization and your own personal goals as well. Your employer may even pick up the bill for training/education, and you might be able to write it off as a tax deduction, too.

Strategy #9: Be Willing to Admit to a Mistake

Whether about a particular situation on the job or even about the job itself, be willing to admit the error of your ways. Only after doing so can you move on to a better place mentally or physically.

Strategy #10: Keep Your Resume Updated

Opportunities come and go in the blink of an eye in business. If you want to be able to respond to those opportunities in a timely fashion, you'll need to keep your resume updated at all times. Just don't update it while you're at work unless you're asked to do so.

Strategy #11: Keep Networking

Networking not only helped you to land this job, but it also will help you to score your next one. Networking is not just for job seekers, however; it is the glue that holds your career together all the time.

Make sure your glue is strong enough by joining professional associations or community organizations. Volunteer for the greater good. Become a respectable community member on such cybersites as Facebook and LinkedIn where you can connect with others who are friends of others or happen to share similar professional interests.

Expand your reach and watch your possibilities grow.

Strategy #12: Work Across Generations Effectively

The working landscape is crowded full of baby boomers, gen Xers, and millennials. Regardless of your age, you will have to work across generations effectively if you are going to be successful on the job today. Working with all these different people may mean that you need to adjust your way of thinking and acting at some point. Do it. We all have something we can learn from each other; we just have to be open to the possibilities in the first place.

Strategy #13: Control Your Digital Dirt

You may be a fine, upstanding example of the perfect employee and the prime candidate for that job promotion. Would your online presence mirror that image? More and more, employers are searching candidates online to see whether something in their personal lives makes them unsuitable for the job. Whether that is legal or fair may be up for debate. It is a reality, however, so control your cyberskeletons and banish them if necessary.

Strategy #14: Be a Company Moneymaker

You bring added financial value to your employer when you introduce new business to the company. By bringing in those bucks, you are showing the Powers That Be that you have the organization's greater interests at heart. For some strange reason, they like that. If business development isn't your favorite pastime, try to get past the pain of sales just long enough to make a positive impression and ensure your place a while longer. In today's environment, this is a priceless skill to call your own.

Strategy #15: Think "Green"

When we say, "Think 'green,'" we don't mean *camouflaged* green, but rather *environmentally* green. Global warming is no longer just the topic of a scary movie, but a genuine concern for all of us. Businesses are feeling the international pressure to quit adding to the destruction of the ozone layer and the extinction of the polar bears and glaciers, among other endangered resources and beings. When you are an employee of one of those businesses, finding cost-effective ways to help your company achieve kudos for playing nice with the world's resources, even on a seemingly small scale, could result in your being credited positively for it on a corporate level.

Strategy #16: Make a Good Thing Better

You don't have to reinvent the wheel on the job to make a good impression. Maybe you just have to tweak it a little bit. Somebody needs to be the one who thinks outside the box within an organization. Maybe that somebody is you. Channel your inner Einstein and become a major creative asset for your boss and your organization as a whole. Who knows? Maybe you'll wind up being the next hottest bubble waiting to burst on the stock market.

The Hardest Thing

The hardest thing for me about leaving the military was losing that inherent trust that comes with the uniform and having to start over earning a reputation as a civilian.

—*Tom Wiederstein, DOD UAV Instructor*

Parting Thoughts

You know that you're not the first person to ever transition from the military in search of a civilian job. This may, however, be the first time *you* have ever faced such an obstacle, and that makes it relevant to you and your family.

Everybody who has gone through this process before has his or her own unique story to tell, just as you will, too. You may look back on your transition with mixed emotions. It is, after all, a bittersweet time in your career and in your life. Either by choice or by force, you are closing the door on one part of your life and opening another one that doesn't always provide a clear picture of what to expect. The unknown can be daunting, to say the least. Your experience while in uniform may have been a good one or not. That depends on how you chose to experience it, just as your transition depends on how you choose to experience it.

> ## To the Future
>
> I look forward to starting my life after the military. Picture your military career as a glass of water that is midway filled. One can look at the glass and say it is half-empty and dwell on the promotion list that you didn't come out on or the job you didn't get or the performance rating that you didn't get that you felt you deserved. I'd rather look at that glass as half full, and look at what water can still go into it. I'm excited about the future, and I have a big smile on my face.
>
> —*Michael L. Holley, U.S. Army, LTC, Retired*

There's no doubt that you won't always have control over the circumstances or the opportunities that may or may not come your way. What you will have control over, however, is how you approach those opportunities. Those who have successfully transitioned before you have done so with an open mind. They allowed themselves the luxury of considering all the alternatives, good and bad. They did not rush decisions that required careful consideration. They asked relevant questions of potential employers and others having knowledge they required. They researched all aspects of the job opportunities using current literature. They listened to what others had to say and then made their decisions based on what was right and beneficial to themselves and their families, regardless of what others might have said or thought.

Just because an opportunity seems to be perfect doesn't mean it is perfect for *you*. It takes great personal courage to filter out the well-meaning voices of those around you and to listen to your own gut. In the end, it is you who will be waking up every day to go to a job you have chosen to accept. You owe it to yourself and your family to be content with your choice. Make a decision. Give it a fighting chance. Do your best. If, after giving it your best shot, you find that the job is not working out, have the sustained courage to look for a new one. You have the tools, knowledge, and experience in doing so already.

Go on. The world is waiting. You've made your mark in uniform, and now it's time to make it as a civilian. If anyone can do it, you can.

APPENDIX

Career Transition Resources

Career Decision Making

About.com: Career Planning
www.careerplanning.about.com

America's Career InfoNet
www.acinet.org/acinet

Career Guide to Industries
www.bls.gov/oco/cg/

Civilian Job News
www.civilianjobnews.com

DOD Dictionary of Military Terms
www.dtic.mil/doctrine/jel/doddict

JobStar
www.jobstar.org

Occupational Outlook Handbook
www.stats.bls.gov/oco/

O*NET
www.onetcenter.org

The Riley Guide
www.rileyguide.com

Salary.com
www.salary.com

Salaryexpert.com
www.salaryexpert.com

Wages, Earning, and Benefits Data
www.stats.bls.gov

Wall Street Journal Job Services
www.careerjournal.com

Education

American Council on Education (ACE) Transfer Guide: Understanding Your Military Credit Recommendations
http://www.acenet.edu/Content/NavigationMenu/ProgramsServices/MilitaryPrograms/Transfer_Guide.htm

CollegeNET
www.collegenet.com

Federal Children Scholarship Fund
www.scholarshipfund.org

GI Bill Information
www.gibill.va.gov

U.S. Department of Education
www.ifap.ed.gov

Employer Research

Annual Report Service
www.annualreportservice.com

BizWeb
www.bizweb.com

Business.com
www.business.com

CEO Express
www.ceoexpress.com

Chambers of Commerce
www.chambers.com

Corporate Information
www.corporateinformation.com

The Corporate Library
www.thecorporatelibrary.com

D&B Million Dollar Database
www.dnbmdd.com/mddi

Forbes Lists
www.forbes.com/lists

Fortune 500
www.fortune.com

Hoovers Online
www.hoovers.com

Internetnews.com
http://stocks.internetnews.com

Moodys
www.moodys.com

Newspapers.com
www.newspapers.com

Standard & Poor's
www2.standardandpoors.com

ThomasNet
www.thomasnet.com

Family

Air Force Crossroads
www.afcrossroads.com

Army Community & Family
Support Center
www.armymwr.com

Army One Source (AOS)
www.ArmyOneSource.com

Army Well-Being Liaison Office
(WBLO)
www.aflo.org

CinCHouse
www.cinchouse.com

Lifelines Quality of Life Mall
www.lifelines.navy.mil

Marine Corps One Source
www.usmc.mil

Military.Com
www.military.com

Military Homefront
www.militaryhomefront.dod.mil

Operation Homefront
www.operationhomefront.net

Federal Employment

Army Civilian Personnel Online
(CPO)
www.cpol.army.mil

Department of Army Civilian
Jobs—Europe
http://cpolrhp.belvoir.army.mil/eur/

Federal Jobs Classifications
www.opm.gov/fedclass/html/
gsseries.htm

Federal Jobs Salary Information
www.opm.gov/oca/payrates

FedWorld
www.fedworld.gov

MWR Army Jobs Online
www.armymwr.com/portal/jobs/

MWR Navy Jobs Online
http://www.mwr.navy.mil/
mwrprgms/personnel.html

U.S. Air Force Civilian Jobs
www.afpc.randolph.af.mil

USAJobs
www.usajobs.opm.gov

U.S. Navy and Marine Corps
Civilian Jobs
https://chart.donhr.navy.mil/

Veterans Employment
Opportunities Act
www.opm.gov/veterans

Veterans Preference Advisor
www.dol.gov/elaws/vetspref.htm

Veterans' Recruitment Authority
(VRA) Wizard
http://cpolrhp.belvoir.army.mil/eur/
employment/vra/index.asp?Try=Yes

Health Care
Deployment Health Support
www.deploymentlink.osd.mil

Retiree Delta Dental Plan
www.ddpdelta.org

Tricare
www.tricare.osd.mil

United Concordia Dental Plan
www.ucci.com

Job Links—Civilian
Bradley-Morris, Inc.
www.bradleymorris.com

Brassring.com
www.brassring.com

CareerBuilder
www.careerbuilder.com

Career.com
www.career.com

CareerOneStop
www.jobbankinfo.org/

Dice (technology jobs)
www.dice.com

EmploymentGuide.com
www.employmentguide.com

Job-Hunt.org
www.job-hunt.org

Job Monkey
www.jobmonkey.com

JobWeb
www.jobweb.com

Monster.com
www.monster.com

NationJob
www.nationjob.com

Vault
www.vault.com

Legislative/Government Agencies
Federal Agency Directory
(Louisiana State University)
www.lib.lsu.edu/gov/index.html

Internal Revenue Service (Tax Info)
www.irs.gov

U.S. Department of Labor Veterans
Employment and Training Service
www.dol.gov/vets/

U.S. House of Representatives
www.house.gov

U.S. Postal Service
www.usps.gov

U.S. Senate
www.senate.gov

U.S. State Department
www.state.gov

Military Associations

Armed Forces Benefit Association
www.afba.com

Association of the U.S. Army
(AUSA)
www.ausa.org

Enlisted Association of the
National Guard
www.eangus.org

The Military Coalition
www.themilitarycoalition.org/

Military Officers Association
www.moaa.org

Military Family Association
www.nmfa.org/

National Guard
www.ngaus.org

Reserve Officers Association
www.roa.org

Military Compensation and Benefits

Military Pay and Entitlements
https://mypay.dfas.mil/mypay.aspx

Personal Benefits Center
www.military.com

Social Security Retirement Planner
www.ssa.gov/retire2/

Thrift Savings Plan
www.tsp.gov

Military Transition

AARTS Transcript (DA Form
5454-R)
https://aartstranscript.army.mil/

Army Career and Alumni Program
www.acap.army.mil

COOL
https://www.cool.army.mil/

Corporate Gray
www.corporategray.com

DOD TransPortal
www.dodtransportal.org

GovBenefits
www.govbenefits.gov

MilitaryHire.com
www.militaryhire.com

Transition Assistance Online
(Times Publishing)
www.taonline.com

TurboTap
www.turbotap.org or www.transitionassistanceprogram.com

VeteransWorld.com
http://www.veteransworld.com/

VetGuide
http://www.opm.gov/veterans/html/
vetguide.asp

VetJobs.com
www.vetjobs.com

VMET (DD Form 2586)
https://www.dmdc.osd.mil/appj/
vmet/index.jsp

News

Air Force News
www.af.mil/news/

Army News
www.dtic.mil/dtic/

Department of Defense News
www.defenselink.mil/news/

Relocation Assistance

HomeFair
www.homefair.com

National Association of Realtors
www.realtor.org

Self-Employment

All Business
www.allbusiness.com

Business.Gov
www.business.gov

Frannet
www.frannet.com

International Franchise Association
www.franchise.org

Small Business Administration
www.sba.gov

World Franchising
www.worldfranchising.com

Service Agencies

Air Force Aid Society
www.afas.org

American Red Cross
http://redcross.org

Armed Forces YMCA
http://asymca.org

Army Emergency Relief
http://www.aerhq.org/

Navy-Marine Corps Relief Society
www.nmcrs.org

World USO
http://uso.org

Veterans and Retirees

American Legion
www.legion.org

Arlington National Cemetery
www.arlingtoncemetery.org

Department of Veterans Affairs Burial & Memorials
www.cem.va.gov

GulfLINK
www.gulflink.osd.mil

Military Handbooks
www.militaryhandbooks.com

Veterans Affairs
www.va.gov

Veterans of Foreign Wars
www.vfw.org

Veterans News & Info Service
www.vnis.com

Voter Information

Federal Voting Assistance Program
www.fvap.gov

Election Assistance Commission
http://www.eac.gov/voter/Register%20to%20Vote

U.S. Military Components

Air Force
www.af.mil

Air Force Reserve
www.afreserve.com/home3.asp

Air National Guard
www.ang.af.mil

Air Reserve Personnel Center
http://afreserve.com/

Army
www.army.mil

Army National Guard
www.arng.army.mil

Army Reserves
http://www.usar.army.mil/arweb/pages/default.aspx

Coast Guard
www.uscg.mil

Coast Guard Personnel Service Center
http://www.uscg.mil/PSC/

Coast Guard Reserve
www.uscg.mil

Employer Support of the Guard & Reserve
www.esgr.org

Guard Family
www.guardfamily.org

Marine Corps
www.usmc.mil

Marine Corps Reserve
www.marforres.usmc.mil

National Guard
http://www.ngb.army.mil/
default.aspx

National Guard Bureau
www.ngb.army.mil

National Guard Virtual Armory
www.virtualarmory.com

Naval Reserve
www.navyreserve.com

Navy
www.navy.mil

Reserve Affairs
www.defenselink.mil/ra/

INDEX

W–Z